All craftsmen share a knowledge

They have held Reality down fluttering to a bench;
Cut wood to their own purposes; compelled
The growth of pattern with the patient shuttle;
Drained acres to a trench.
Control is theirs. They have ignored the subtle
Release of spirit from the jail of shape.
They have been concerned with prison, not escape;
Pinioned the fact, and let the rest go free,
And out of need made inadvertent art.
All things designed to play a faithful part
Build up their plain particular poetry.
Tools have their own integrity;

the sneath of scythe curves rightly to the hand,
The hammer knows its balance, knife its edge,
All tools inevitably planned,
Stout friends, with pledge
Of service, with their crotchets too
That masters understand,
And proper character, and separate heart,
But always to their chosen temper true.

Much goes to little making,— law and skill,
Tradition's usage, each man's separate gift;
Till the slow worker sees that he has wrought
More than he knew of builded truth,
As one who slips through years of youth,
Leaving his young indignant rage,
And finds the years' insensible drift
Brings him achievement with the truce of age.

The above passage is written for JHAND HRCOLM from "The Land," by V. Sackville-West.

1949
Vellum manufacturers,
Plough yard Brentford SCRIBE

Not that they beggare

that they have chosen

In lonely places: but t

to the high stars, the

Freedom they seek, an

From worthless hopes,

And all the noisy crow

And whatsoever war:

At Christ's comman

to Ausonius

translation by
Helen Waddell

e in mind, or brutes,

ir dwelling place afar

r eyes are turned

deep of Truth.

ptiness apart

of the marketplace,

ng up of things,

the divine,

nd for His love, they hate

MORE THAN FINE WRITING

The Life and Calligraphy of
Irene Wellington

MORE THAN FINE WRITING

The Life and Calligraphy of Irene Wellington

HEATHER CHILD
HEATHER COLLINS
ANN HECHLE
DONALD JACKSON

THE BRITISH LIBRARY

The re-publication of this book has been made
possible by financial contributions from the
Crafts Study Centre Trust, the Pilgrim Trust,
The Scriveners' Company and the
Irene Wellington Educational Trust.

First published in Great Britain in 1986 by Pelham Books

This edition published 1998 by
The British Library
96 Euston Road
London NW1 2DB

ISBN 0 7123 4605 8

Origination by Grafiscan, Verona
Printed in Hong Kong by South Sea International Press

CONTENTS

Acknowledgements

Essentially this book is a tribute to Irene Wellington and tangible proof of the hard work and dedication she was able to inspire. We are indebted to Heather Child, Heather Collins, Ann Hechle and Donald Jackson who have all given their time and expertise to make this publication a reality. Many months of research and patient cataloguing by Heather Collins of the Irene Wellington Collection in the Crafts Study Centre, Holburne Museum, Bath, provided a solid background for much of the writing. This research was made possible by financial assistance from the Irene Wellington Collection Appeal, the Society of Scribes and Illuminators and the Trustees of the Crafts Study Centre. Justin Howes has been a most valuable aid and critic in the course of the work, and thanks are also due to Rhod Bass, Jean Bushby, Mary Nicholson, Robert Wellington, the Dowager Marchioness of Cholmondeley, and the many others who contributed memories and details of Irene's life.

The majority of illustrations which contribute so greatly to the book were taken by Peter Hutchings from manuscripts in the Crafts Study Centre Collection. We are also grateful to Michael Dudley, Brian Hebditch and Colin Wilson for photographing work further afield, and to the many individuals and institutions who have kindly given permission for the work to be photographed and reproduced as detailed below.

The works on the following pages are reproduced by kind permission of: Crafts Study Centre, pages 1–3, 48, 54 (*top*), 55 (*bottom*), 56–8, 60, 63–6 (*top*), 67–9, 72–5, 77 (*bottom*), 78–80, 82–3 (*left*), 85–7, 92–5, 101–3, 118–19 (*top, centre*), 120–21, 124, 126–32, 142–4 (*bottom*); Irene Wellington Educational Trust, pages 17–18, 21, 23, 26, 45, 49, 53–4 (*centre, bottom*), 55 (*top*), 66 (*bottom right*), 133 (*centre, bottom*); Christ Church Library, pages 70–1, 108–9; The Dowager Marchioness of Cholmondeley, pages 90–1, 96–7, 112–13; Bodleian Library, Oxford, page 119 (*bottom*), Ms. Dou. d. 136; Bodleian Library, Oxford and Marie Angel, pages 116–17, Ms. Dou, d. 136; Donald Jackson, pages 46–7, 51; Andrew Johnston, pages 62, 81; Andrew Johnston and A & C Black (Publishers) Ltd, page 59; Lydd Town Council, pages 106–7, 122–3; Newberry Library, Chicago, courtesy of the John M. Wing Foundation, pages 114–15; Vatican Library, Rome, page 29; Victoria and Albert Museum, London, page 61; The Warden and Fellows of Winchester College, pages 98–100; Association Typographique, pages 133 (*top*), 144 (*top*); Minnesota Manuscript Initiative, pages 66 (*bottom left*), 83 (*top, bottom right*), 84; Society of Scribes and Illuminators, pages 125, 134; pages 88–9 from *The Irene Wellington Copy Book*, Omnibus Edition (Taplinger Publishing Co, Inc: New York, 1980), used by permission; the works on pages 104–5 and 110–11 are reproduced by the gracious permission of Her Majesty the Queen.

The photographs on pages 46–9, 51, 54–60, 62–5, 66 (*top*), 67–69, 72–5, 77 (*bottom*), 78–82, 83 (*left*), 85–9, 93–5, 101–3, 118–19, 124–34 were taken by Peter Hutchings; pages 1–3, 66 (*bottom left*), 83 (*top, bottom right*), 84, 90–1, 96–100, 104–5, 110–13, 120–1, 142–4 by Colin Wilson; pages 70–1, 108–9 by Michael Dudley; pages 106–7 by Brian Hebditch.

BARLEY ROSCOE
Curator, Crafts Study Centre,
Holburne Museum, Bath

INTRODUCTION

Irene Wellington is widely acknowledged as one of the most distinguished and influential figures in the development of calligraphy this century. She was a talented student of Edward Johnston at the Royal College of Art, London, in the 1920s and devoted much of her life to furthering his work. Through the quality of her own penmanship and as a teacher of rare distinction, Irene is a vital link in the tradition of modern craftsmanship, between Johnston's teaching methods and practice and the range of calligraphic work being done world-wide today.

This book illustrates the particular scope of Irene's calligraphy and illumination, with examples drawn mainly from the extensive collection of her work at the Crafts Study Centre, Bath. The illustrated section on her work traces the development of her art from the early student studies at the RCA, the notebooks of Johnston's lectures, finished manuscripts and rough drafts of important commissions to more informal pieces written out for her own pleasure and as gifts to friends. Fortunately, throughout her working life Irene kept the many rough drafts and sketches she made of her illuminated manuscripts, and the Crafts Study Centre has become the beneficiary.

At a memorial meeting held in 1945 to pay tribute to Edward Johnston, Irene said: 'I personally owe all I know of lettering to his lead, and beyond that, and more than that, I learned from *what he was*. We scribes of today, directly or indirectly, look upon him *as master*.'[1] Many scribes have followed the Johnston tradition, but few like Irene – while being essentially herself – have captured his spirit in their own work. Reproductions do not convey the subtleties of penmanship, or the tactile qualities of materials; only the study of original manuscripts can reveal what Johnston meant when he wrote: 'The excellence and beauty of Formal Penmanship is achieved chiefly by three things – SHARPNESS, UNITY & FREEDOM.'[2] These essential qualities are fully expressed in the remarkable rhythm, vitality and sensitive touch of Irene's calligraphy and make her manuscripts truly the work of a poet.

HEATHER CHILD
December 1985

[1] *Tributes to Edward Johnston* privately printed 1948
[2] *Writing & Illuminating, & Lettering* Edward Johnston 1906

SETTING THE SCENE

THE REVIVAL OF
CALLIGRAPHY

When Edward Johnston came to London as a young man in 1897, with the intention of 'going in for art', the calligraphic skills had long been forgotten, superseded by the invention and spread of printing in the fifteenth and early sixteenth centuries. Through his scholarly studies of historical manuscripts Johnston rediscovered the essential principles on which formal writing with the edged-pen had been based and gave the craft a new and contemporary meaning. He exemplified William Morris's ideal of research into the arts of the past:

> Let us study it wisely, be taught by it, kindled by it; all the while determining not to imitate or repeat it; to have either no art at all, or an art which we have made our own.[1]

Johnston produced work of superb quality himself and laid the foundation of a school of calligraphy that led the international revival of this century. By the turn of the century the interest in his teaching at the newly formed Central School of Arts and Crafts was already extending outwards.

Before the invention of the printing press around the mid-fifteenth century, there was a long unbroken tradition of writing books by hand on papyrus, parchment or paper. Consequently, the aim of the early printer was to produce books closely resembling those written by the professional scribes. The subsequent centuries saw a decline in standards of formal penmanship. Many professional scribes became writing masters; they produced handsome, engraved copy-books in which to display their skills and to teach them to others. During the eighteenth and early nineteenth centuries the professional scribes – scriveners and law-writers – were still a necessary part of every-day life; they used a copperplate script of the engraver, written with a fine quill and later with the pointed metal pens that came into general use after the 1830s. The printing press did not immediately kill the art of illumination, and manuscripts such as grants of nobility, letters patent and diplomas continue to this day to be written and richly decorated by professional scribes and illuminators.

At the time when Johnston began to study early manuscripts, there were some curious beliefs concerning the actual making of individual letter-forms. Enthusiastic Victorians, with an ecclesiastical interest in illuminated texts, copied medieval and Gothic letters

---

[1] *The Lesser Arts* William Morris 1878

in outline with a mapping-pen, then painstakingly filled the space between the lines with a brush, thereby missing the spontaneous gesture essential to fine writing. It became clear to Johnston, who as a boy had also written out texts on Sundays, that the mapping-pen and the brush were not the way forward.

The introduction to England of colour-printing by chromolithography in the 1830s revolutionised the art of the book. Magnificent illuminated volumes were produced by Henry Shaw, Owen Jones and Noel Humphreys, illustrating pages from early and medieval manuscripts with varying degrees of accuracy. These were followed by popular books on illumination which usually contained plates drawn in outline for hand-colouring, and primers containing chromolitho reproductions of illuminated initials and decorative borders. This was the period of the growing Gothic revival in architecture, which became popular also in Europe and America, with its romantic concept of medievalism.

As a result, the calligraphic revival became associated with overtones of dubious medievalism that persisted into the early twentieth century:

> The enthusiasm for the art of illumination generated by Owen Jones, Noel Humphreys and their collaborators and imitators created a small body of informed but largely antiquarian taste. It did not have much influence on the art of lettering as practised up and down the country: no artist of originality made lettering his special field or made any important contribution to formal lettering or type design in Britain until William Morris, aided by Emery Walker, founded the Kelmscott Press in 1891. Morris himself practised the writing and illumination of manuscripts in the early 1870s and bought and studied original manuscripts.[1]

The inventions of photographic block-making and mechanical composition hastened the end of handcrafts in book production, resulting in a visual decline in the quality of printed books generally. By the end of the nineteenth century the standard of typography in ordinary books was extremely low and craftsmanship passed to the major private presses, which were concerned, as they are today, to control quality to a high degree in the production of books with fine typography, fine paper and bindings.

Johnston acknowledged the debt owed to Morris in pointing the way to the practical revival of calligraphy. In 1908 he wrote:

> William Morris was the first person in England to revive the art of writing and illuminating, as he revived so many other arts, on the lines established by the ancient masters. Several books are in existence exquisitely written and decorated by him, notably a Horace, a Vergil and two differently treated copies of Omar Khayyam.[2]

The Arts and Crafts revival, inspired by Ruskin and Morris in protest against the shoddiness of industrialism, was at its height when Johnston came to London bringing

[1] *Victorian Book Design and Colour Printing* Ruari McLean 1963
[2] *Writing & Illuminating, & Lettering* Edward Johnston 2nd ed 1908

with him an introduction to the architect William Cowlishaw, for whom illumination was a passionate interest. Johnston soon came to meet people influential in the Arts and Crafts Movement, notably Sydney Cockerell who had been Morris's secretary, and W. R. Lethaby, a younger friend of Morris, both of whom encouraged Johnston to study historical manuscripts.

William Richard Lethaby, born in 1857, architect, designer and educationalist, was a founder of the Central School of Arts and Crafts and its first Principal; he believed that crafts were a vital necessity within an industrialised society. In choosing staff for his new school he drew on contacts with the Arts and Crafts Movement, through his membership of the Art Workers Guild founded in 1884 and the Arts and Crafts Exhibition Society in 1888.

One of Lethaby's most brilliant appointments was that of Edward Johnston, who had visited him in 1898 as a young student of calligraphy. To his own astonishment, Johnston soon found himself in charge of the new class in writing and illuminating at the Central. These must have been some of the most exciting classes in the school, as Johnston did not attempt to hide from his students the fact that he was himself gradually (and with constant encouragement and advice from Lethaby) recreating the techniques of the craft. Johnston's influence was enormous: brilliant young students such as Noel Rooke and Eric Gill claimed that Johnston altered the whole course of their lives; foreign pupils returned to open classes in Johnston's tradition in their own countries and he was particularly influential in Germany. His impact on book production and print-making was profound. In the trajectory of Johnston's career, from his study of medieval manuscripts in the British Museum to the designing of his block-letter alphabet for the London Underground, we find the embodiment of Lethaby's vision of the relationship of handcraft to modern society. The calligraphy and illuminating classes were perhaps the most dramatic example of this mission to revive lost or dying crafts and pass them on to a younger generation; similar circumstances, however, could be found throughout the School: May Morris's instruction in embroidery, the extremely popular classes in bookbinding using tools made by Douglas Cockerell himself, Alexander Fisher's revitalising of the art of enamelling and the exciting classes in colour wood-block printing based on Japanese techniques pioneered by Frank Morley Fletcher.[1]

In 1901 Lethaby was appointed Professor of Ornament and Design at the Royal College of Art and in the same year Johnston also began his part-time teaching of lettering there. In the 1920s Irene Wellington attended Johnston's classes and in 1927 became his assistant in the writing class.

Among Lethaby's seminal activities was the planning and editing of *The Artistic Crafts Series of Technical Handbooks* in which Johnston's classic manual *Writing &*

---

[1] *W. R. Lethaby and the Central School* Theresa Gronberg 1984

Illuminating, & Lettering first appeared in 1906 and which has been in print ever since. It is difficult to exaggerate the importance of this series of books on the development of the crafts at the beginning of this century.

During the last fifteen years of his life Johnston worked on a second book: *Formal Penmanship* which was left unfinished when he died. In due course this important material was edited for publication by the present writer. Irene's perceptive understand/ing of Johnston's teaching and her grasp of the philosophy underlying all his work enabled her to clarify the more obscure passages in his manuscript. The book was published in time to coincide with the Johnston Centenary exhibition at the RCA in 1972, a major event for which Irene had been one of the organisers. She did not live to see the publication of *Lessons in Formal Writing*, 1986, a companion volume to *Formal Penmanship*, but she took an active interest in its progress and wrote a charming piece for inclusion recollecting some of Johnston's sayings.

It is a happy outcome that brings the extensive archive of Edward Johnston's work, donated to the Crafts Study Centre in 1985 by his family, into juxtaposition with the unique Irene Wellington collection. These important collections constitute a calli/graphic resource of international importance – a mine of information for students, an inspiration for practising calligraphers and all those who are 'at heart desirous to quicken the arts.'

HEATHER CHILD

IRENE WELLINGTON

A BACKGROUND

Tourney Hall was a large farmhouse set amongst thirty acres of mixed farming land, close to the bleak and windswept marshes of Lydd, on the Kent coast. Here, on 29 October 1904, Charles and Julia Bass's ninth – and last – child was born: a daughter, Irene. A true farmer's child, she was brought up free to roam the local fields, which instilled in her a love and sympathy with the world of nature that was never to leave her. As soon as she was old enough, she earned extra pocket money by helping with the various farm jobs that had to be carried out each season and, like her brothers and sisters, took her turn at separating the milk before breakfast. Life revolved round the farm and family, and apart from an occasional Sunday School outing, the children rarely went further than Lydd. The family were keen Methodists – Charles Bass was a Minister – and the Chapel and local school were the major outside influences of Irene's early years.

Irene in school uniform

From the age of eleven, Irene and her sister Rose boarded at Ashford County School, returning home at weekends. At that time, Irene's main interest was in sport; she won several tennis trophies, and wanted to become a games mistress, but wasn't thought to have the necessary stamina. Her other interests, which were to continue throughout her life, were English and drawing.

In 1921 Irene began a broad-based art course at Maidstone School of Art. It was there that she first learned lettering, taught by Arthur Sharp, and became fascinated and absorbed by it, returning after the classes ended to work alone. She was introduced to Edward Johnston's *Writing &*

18

Illuminating, & Lettering, and in 1925 won a Royal Exhibition scholarship to the Royal College of Art in London, where Johnston was teaching one day a week. Although she chose to specialise in calligraphy, the RCA course, like the one at Maidstone, covered a wide range of subjects, including textile design, embroidery, architecture and printmaking.

Her first years at the RCA were not easy ones for Irene. At Maidstone School of Art she had been one of the most talented pupils, and had passed several subjects with distinction. She now found herself just one of many gifted students. Previously, she had been completing fully illuminated and gilded manuscripts, but found herself, under Johnston's tuition, returning to the fundamentals of lettering, and having to re-learn basic forms from the beginning. The unaccustomed freedom of art-school life in itself proved to be highly disturbing. The contrast between these new values and her strict Methodist upbringing became too much for Irene to accept and during her second year at the RCA she suffered a very severe nervous breakdown. Her place on the course was kept open for her by the Bursar, the painter Hubert Wellington (who, almost twenty years later, was to become her second husband). She returned to the College after a year, at the end of which she gained her diploma, despite her long absence.

Irene remained at the RCA for a further two years, in the final one covering teacher training. From 1927 she was Johnston's assistant in the writing class. She had a perceptive understanding of his teaching, and said of him much later: 'He was, of anyone I have ever met, the one to have the *strongest influence* on me, in both my life and my work. I learned from what he was.'

In 1929 Irene was elected a Craft Member of the Society of Scribes and Illuminators, which had been formed in 1921 for 'the advancement of the crafts of Writing and Illuminating by the practice of them for themselves alone'. In 1930 she completed her formal training and left the RCA.

In September of the same year, she married a cousin whom she had long admired: Ernest John (Jack) Sutton. Jack was an income-tax officer in Edinburgh, and Irene moved there to join him. Almost immediately, she began her first major commission, The Oxfordshire and Buckinghamshire Light Infantry Roll of Honour for the First World War, which took her almost a year to complete. She also carried out smaller pieces of work, for clients and friends.

Irene was also teaching. Hubert Wellington had by then become Principal of Edinburgh College of Art, and, in a letter to him, Edward Johnston recommended Irene as a teacher. She was, he said, unusually well fitted to the task, and had executed some exceptionally fine pieces of work. Irene herself had misgivings about teaching, but, despite this, in 1932 became a part-time instructor of writing and illuminating at the College. Her classes were small — no more than a dozen students — which meant she could teach individually rather than by lectures and general demonstrations.

OPPOSITE
ABOVE: Tourney Hall, Lydd. BELOW: The Bass family *c.* 1909; (Irene in centre, between her parents)

Most of the students had done a year's work already, and had 'things to unlearn'. They wrote with steel nibs and between two lines. Irene insisted that, in the interests of freedom in the writing, they use one line only, and she started the most promising pupils with quills. Her teaching was much on the lines of Johnston in the importance placed on 'The Thing': the piece of work itself. She wrote to him about her classes: 'I hope that we shall be able to stir them up to produce something free and vigorous and that their letters will flourish – but not unduly – and that they will enjoy it.'

Meanwhile, away from Johnston's direct influence, and cut off from the mainstream of calligraphy, Irene's own very personal and lively style of calligraphy was forming. Although not obvious to her at the time, Irene felt later that this period of relative isolation had been good for her art, allowing her own ideas to develop. From Johnston she had learned the importance of a thorough understanding of the craft and its traditions; but in working alone and in having to think for herself, she gradually developed a highly personal way of expressing her chosen texts, in what was then a very unorthodox manner. Her sensitive interpretation of Johnston's teaching, coupled with her own search for the truth, were combining to give her work a unique and individual direction.

As the years passed, Irene was forced to admit to herself that her marriage to Jack was not a success. Apart from their background, they seemed to have had little in common. He was very much involved in a local Methodist group, and although Irene would accompany him to meetings, and on occasion give talks on calligraphy and lettering, the Methodist Chapel was no longer an important feature in her life. For his part, Jack's interests did not lie in the artistic world, and he gave Irene little encouragement in her work. His reserved personality and strictly organised life-style did not blend well with his wife's intuitive, sensitive and often indecisive nature. Communication between them became increasingly difficult. At times Irene escaped into her work, becoming totally absorbed by it; but sometimes she was so deeply depressed that she could not work at all, and by 1938 said that she had done little work for a year and had 'come to rather a bleak patch'. Nervous breakdowns threatened her again, but she was fortunate in having made in Edinburgh several staunch friends who gave her much needed support during those difficult years.

One of the closest of these friends was Charlotte Wellington, Hubert's wife. It was for her that Irene carried out one of her most delicate pieces of work: a small birthday card on vellum, transcribing lines from Robert Bridges' 'The Testament of Beauty' ('Deep springs of happiness'). She combined the use of a crow quill for the writing with a brush for the illustration of a violet: a daring combination of techniques at that time.

However, in February 1942, after a brief illness, Charlotte died. The shock of her death brought Hubert and Irene closer together, and in sharing their grief, they fell in love.

Within a few weeks of his wife's death, Hubert decided to retire and move down to Henley on Thames, to The White House, which he and Charlotte had already

The White House

begun to rent for holidays. When he left Edinburgh College of Art at the end of the summer term, the staff presented him with a leather-bound 'Appreciation' which Irene had devised, written and illustrated. It was a happy combination of the formal and the personal: there were drawings of both the College and The White House, and amongst a selection of spring flowers was the violet which had appeared on Charlotte's birthday card earlier that year.

Irene continued to teach at Edinburgh College of Art. The staffroom was used by fire-watchers during the wartime air-raids, and every few weeks she would write out a large panel to pin on the wall 'to encourage and inspire' and 'give mental nourish-ment'. The texts were carefully chosen; many were taken from Robert Bridges' 'The Testament of Beauty', and V. Sackville-West's 'The Land'. Both poems were to pro-vide Irene with material for her work for many more years.

In the meantime, Irene's domestic situation had not improved, and she envisaged it becoming increasingly difficult now that Jack, who was considerably older than she was, had begun to make plans for his retirement; the prospect of them both being at home together for much of the day appalled Irene, and it became obvious to her that she could no longer continue with the pretence of a happy marriage. She had no wish to hurt Jack, but her own integrity and insistence on honesty in all things made it impossible for her to continue with the relationship, which had become a shallow, and often infuriating, one for both of them. She was also unhappy about the deception involved in concealing her deepening feelings for Hubert. She and Hubert corresponded almost every day, sometimes twice a day, and in her letters Irene was able to give vent to the deep frustrations she felt about her inhibited life-style. Hubert shared the same values that she did, and offered her advice and encouragement, and

Irene realised that in him she had found the mutual love and respect which were missing from her marriage.

The strengthening bond with Hubert, and his support, made Irene's decision about her marriage easier. In the summer of 1943, but still only after a great struggle of conscience, she decided to leave Jack and return to London. For a week she stayed in a Bloomsbury hotel, but was soon found a room in a flat in Primrose Hill belonging to a friend of Hubert and Charlotte's younger son, Robert. He was also instrumental in arranging for her to have a small space in the corner of an architect's office, where she could continue to work. She had brought several small commissions with her from Edinburgh, and she completed these whilst starting to build the foundations of her new life.

Before she left Edinburgh, Irene had put in a petition for the annulment of her marriage, and in September of the following year it was granted. Two months later she married Hubert Wellington, and moved into The White House. This was the beginning of the time which she spoke of as the happiest of her life. Irene and Hubert shared a studio, converted from an old stable, at the side of the house. Hubert valued her work, and gradually helped her regain confidence in both herself and her art; he provided the secure background from which she could go forward.

In the next fifteen years Irene Wellington's work reached its full flowering and maturity. She executed such formal works as The Oxfordshire and Buckinghamshire Light Infantry Roll of Honour for the Second World War, written with a confidence and individuality lacking in its companion volume, which had shown a strong John‑stonian influence; The Wykehamist Roll of Honour, with its elegantly designed title page and sensitively drawn angels; and the Accession and Coronation Addresses presented by the London County Council to Queen Elizabeth II. As in Irene's other formal work, while always handled in a suitably dignified manner, her own liveliness of touch is keenly, but subtly, visible. Having discovered that the new sovereign was fond of horses – as was Irene, who had included them in many of her designs since childhood – she at first thought of incorporating them in the Coronation Address, leaping through foliage, in the style of Eastern manuscripts. But she decided that although this might appeal to the Queen, the idea was too light‑hearted, and so she settled for a more formal approach, transcribing the dedicatory speech made by Princess Elizabeth after her father's death. Irene thought the Queen might be pleased to find this speech had been noted and remembered.

During her years at The White House Irene also carried out many informal pieces of work, often as gifts for friends. She thought of these as being amongst her best work, as she had no restrictions placed on her, and felt free to include any touches of humour she thought the recipient might appreciate. During the 1940s she had been introduced to Lord Cholmondeley by Sydney Cockerell, and had given him lessons in italic handwriting. She sent a personal card to him, taking as its title Eckhart's 'Just like one who wants to learn to write', which opened out into seven sections, each showing an example of a different style of writing. Both Lord and Lady

Irene and Hubert

Cholmondeley became good friends. After receiving a turkey from their Norfolk estate one Christmas, Irene's spontaneous response was to send them a complex and vigorously illustrated double opening – 'Upon being given a Norfolk Turkey' – written 'in the spare time of 3 days'.

On other occasions Irene would struggle for a long time over much simpler pieces, unable to resolve them to her satisfaction. She had never been happy with the way her contribution to Alfred Fairbank's *A Book of Scripts* – a stanza from T. S. Eliot's 'Little Gidding' – had been reproduced, and when the book was revised, she was given the opportunity of replacing the piece with something else. She chose to transcribe a much shorter passage, only seven lines long. It was a quotation by Professor E. A. Lowe, beginning 'Calligraphy is distinguished by harmony of style.' By writing in a much larger and bolder hand, Irene hoped the piece would retain its sharpness and sensitivity of touch in reproduction. She completed the quotation at least a dozen times, finding fault with details which to others appeared perfect. Later she made notes about some of the rejected versions, explaining why they had failed to meet the demands she made on them. The integrity which was fundamental to her character was evident in her methods of work: she could not allow a lowering of standards. She must produce the best she knew herself capable of. Her work mirrored what she was: her sensitivity, humour, dedication and depth of thinking were visible both in her choice of text and its execution. Underlying this, lay strong spiritual values.

Irene's beliefs posed problems as well as providing comfort. Hubert was a Roman Catholic, and Irene considered joining the Catholic Church. She was no longer aligned to any particular religious body, but felt there to be something about Catholicism which was not right for her personally. It was a dilemma which surfaced again and again over the following years. Although she had always thought of herself as having a strong spiritual sense, sometimes she was filled with doubts about whether this was really so. Gradually, she realised that each time she was close to an emotional breakdown, a recurrent problem throughout her life, it was related to religious feelings. She tried to resolve some of her doubts on paper, jotting down her thoughts in notebooks, being thoroughly honest with herself. At times she would find herself grateful for the painful experiences of life, which she felt – or hoped – would make her less likely to be critical of others; but on other occasions she passed through what she termed 'periods of blank frustration' when she could see no benefit resulting from her depression.

The physical act of writing was important to Irene, whether carried out with a carefully prepared quill or one of her many different coloured biros; it seemed as if her thoughts crystallised on paper rather than in her mind, and that self-expression came more easily through the written word. She kept numerous notebooks, where the mundane mingled with her ponderings on Truth and God. Shopping lists and menus were interwoven with thoughts on the way she felt or worked: 'I work more by impulse, feeling, emotion. Innocent enthusiasm. Personal things. Copying in excitement. Shattering periods of conscious assessment. Gradual personal consolidation.' In conversation she could be very articulate, but was slow, often needing long silences when she could formulate her thoughts. If she was asked to give a talk, she would plan it with the same deliberation and attention to detail which she gave to her calligraphy. Words were deleted, altered, and often reinstated. She would sometimes write in the margin why one choice seemed better than another, in order to clarify her final decision, or perhaps to help her make it.

Of her teaching, Irene noted: 'Teaching in belief; teaching in question.' In September 1944 she accepted the part-time job which Noel Rooke offered her at the Central School of Arts and Crafts in London. She continued as an instructor there for the next fifteen years. She had never wanted to teach, and still frequently found it exhausting and a strain. But she felt that she could – and therefore should – help to promote the craft by passing on the techniques and discipline, and by revealing its inherent possibilities. Her approach was a personal one, going to endless trouble to find exactly the right reference material and historic examples for individual students. But her slow and searching methods of teaching, suggesting projects well beyond the student's capability, constantly re-evaluating the work and recommending further changes, did not suit everyone. A lot of what she said was not understood. As Johnston had demanded the best from his students, Irene did from hers. And like him, she had the ability to criticise in such a perceptive and constructive way that the student was encouraged to go on, having been awakened to their own further potential. During her final years at the Central School, Ann Hechle and Donald Jackson were amongst her students. Both have since said that much of Irene's teaching was lost on them at the time, and it is only in the intervening years that they have recognised the importance and relevance of what she taught.

Irene's teaching was never limited to the classroom. Many of her acquaintances acknowledge a debt to her for altering their perception of the whole field of lettering. She also made three attempts to write books, but of these only the series of Copybooks was published. The other two, far more complex in character, were never completed. And the Copybooks, like so much of her work, show only the tip of a very large iceberg; after she had selected the writing to go into them, three folders of rejects remained, inches high, along with her customary 'working thoughts' which filled further sheets of paper. The finished book gives only a small indication of the hours of work and the depth of thought and effort involved. The same is true of the title page for 'Quartet of the Seasons' – a manuscript book illustrated by Marie Angel and written by Irene Wellington – in which a highly detailed idea is gradually pared down to a very simple design.

By the 1960s, Hubert, who was twenty-five years older than Irene, was in failing health and occasionally in hospital. But most of the time he was at home, being nursed by Irene; he found his failing faculties hard to accept, and she tried to give him what encouragement and help she could. As he needed more attention, Irene did less calligraphic work, and the quality of the few things she did complete at that time show the strain she was under. In 1967 Hubert died, and Irene had to try and adjust to a life without the person who had been her strongest support.

After years when her domestic affairs had taken priority, Irene now had to re-assess her life. She was offered a mews flat in Kensington by Lady Cholmondeley, and in 1969 she left The White House and moved to London, where she began to work and take on commissions again. In 1972 she started what was to be her last major piece of work: The Bailiffs of Lydd, a commemorative panel which now hangs in the Guildhall there. Its companion piece is The Borough of Lydd, a panel which Irene had written in 1948 in memory of her father, who had twice been Mayor of the Borough. She found the Bailiffs a struggle, and at times was helped by younger calligraphers in the preparation of the vellum, the tracings, and even with some of the painted lettering. But the design and calligraphy were her own, demonstrating her distinctive style and bearing witness to a long and thorough knowledge of her subject; recent trends in the craft, however, were reflected in the juxtaposition of the built-up capitals at the top of the panel.

Irene had always remained open to outside influences; she had never stopped learning, and in 1971–2 she was attending palaeography classes, taught in the evenings by Professor Julian Brown of the University of London. Again, she was making her comprehensive and thoughtful notes, pondering over what she had learned; after

Irene at Steep, *c.* 1974

a lesson on rustic capitals, she produced a well-considered sheet of examples, in both pen and double-pencils, with a translation of the Latin text and notes on the construction of the forms. She was the most assiduous of students.

In 1974 Irene decided to leave London; she moved to Steep, in Hampshire, where her stepson Robert had offered her a home. Two years later she returned to her birthplace at Lydd, to share her brother's house, built on a site which had once formed part of their father's farm. Her output had dwindled, due in part to illness and a period in hospital, but when she could, she continued to work on an oval panel which she had been planning since she had lived in London. It was to be an illustrated piece of work, based on Gerard Manley Hopkins' sonnet 'As kingfishers catch fire, dragon‚ flies draw flame', a poem which had always moved her in its sentiments of all things fulfilling their own purpose in life: 'What I do is me: for that I came.' She was hindered by failing sight, and laboured over the work. The piece was never completed.

In 1982 Irene's working life came to an abrupt halt when she suffered a stroke. After three months in hospital, she spent two years in a nursing home: difficult years, when, being unable to write, and finding it painful to speak, communication became almost impossible. For long periods she found it hard to know how to fill her days, and at other times she was only aware of the severe and constant pain she was in. She felt she had nothing left to offer. But, in being thrown back on solely her own inner resources, and despite periods of quiet desperation, Irene's spiritual belief and faith became deeper. She entered the Catholic Church in 1984, and died on 18 Septem‚ ber in the same year.

But those qualities which profoundly affected many who came into contact with Irene — her integrity, the depth of her thinking, her humour, the humble approach to her craft, and the sheer joy she experienced from writing — live on in her art. She devoted herself to her work, and it remains an embodiment of what she was. The sensitivity which caused her deepest doubts was the root from which her best work sprang. She risked facing her deepest emotions, as few are willing to do, and in return she experienced life in its fullest sense, from its heights to its depths; tears flowed readily from her, but they could as easily be tears of happiness as tears of despair. In her work, as in her life, the goals she set herself were so high that the vision necessarily remained slightly out of reach, still to be grasped in the future. But the striving towards perfection, towards the true meaning behind all things, was all important. For Irene, the ultimate failure would have been not to make that attempt at all. The search for truth — whatever it might bring — was an integral part of life and of being alive. Her struggles have been our gain.

HEATHER COLLINS

IRENE WELLINGTON IN THE CONTEXT OF HER TIME

A PERSONAL VIEW

When I once confessed to Irene that I found it hard to give myself to my work as a calligrapher because it seemed meaningless in a world so full of torment and uncertainty, she reminded me of Johnston's quotation from Emerson in *Writing & Illuminating, & Lettering*:

> We must set up the strong present tense against all the rumours of wrath, past or to come. So many things are unsettled which it is of the first importance to settle, – and, pending their settlement, we will do as we do. . . . Expediency of literature, reason of literature, lawfulness of writing down a thought, is questioned; much is to say on both sides, and, while the fight waxes hot, thou, dearest scholar, stick to thy foolish task, add a line every hour, and between whiles add a line. . . . Thou art sick, but shalt not be worse, and the universe, which holds thee dear, shall be the better.[1]

Then, I took it to mean that I must get on with what I knew best while I could, but it has another meaning: setting up a 'strong present tense' also implies that what we make must speak for its own time. Irene herself wrote that 'handwriting is always an expression of its own culture. A living thing – which writing is – must grow, change and be renewed if it is to stay alive.'[2]

Irene was always proud to acknowledge her debt to Johnston, but she was able to admire him without abdicating responsibility for her own ideas. Where other people may have been content merely to repeat what they learnt from him, she was able to take him at his word and prove that 'Rules are there to be used as a spring-board for right and lively work, *not* for rigidity but for liberation: rules and laws so comprehended as to be rightly used – or consciously overruled –in the right spirit.'

The importance for Irene, and for us, of calligraphy being of the present, of its own time, can only be appreciated against the background of the revival of calligraphy in the nineteenth century as part of the Arts and Crafts movement in England and contemporary movements in the crafts and architecture of Europe – in particular Germany. These movements led to the establishment of schools of arts and crafts which provided training in writing, illuminating and lettering and continue to influence generations of students in Europe and America to this day.

[1] Ralph Waldo Emerson, quoted in *Writing & Illuminating, & Lettering*
[2] *Dossier A–Z* (Association Typographique) Belgium 1973

THE GOSPEL OF ST MARK

English; eighth century; freely drawn on vellum with a quill pen and using various drawing
instruments, such as compasses and ruler.
34 × 35 cm (whole page); detail illustrated of initial letter beginning the Gospel of St Mark
approximately 17 × 12.5 cm

A scribe, probably working in England, has combined images and designs from Irish and Anglo-
Saxon cultures and from Classical sources to produce an initial letter unique to his own time and
place. In the same way, Irene Wellington used the work of past artists as a springboard for inspiration
and ideas.

In the wake of the enormous success of the 'Great Exhibition of Works of Industry of all Nations' in 1851, which highlighted industry's need for trained designers, schools of 'Arts and Crafts' were established throughout the United Kingdom with the support of such powerful champions of the industrial age as Prince Albert. But, like the Victoria and Albert Museum and its sister institution the Royal College of Art, they were soon influenced by the ideas of John Ruskin and William Morris who rejected the products of the machine in favour of things made by 'one man for another'. One aspect of Ruskin's new order was an imaginative and idealistic reconstruction of the craft guilds of the fourteenth-century. Ruskin's thought had inspired William Morris as an undergraduate at Oxford in the 1850s, and through him Cockerell, Lethaby and ultimately Johnston.

The Central School of Arts and Crafts was founded in 1896. W. R. Lethaby, its first principal, believed that 'beauty can only be brought back to common life by doing common work in an interesting way'[1] and that this beauty should be part of the daily life of everyone. It was not a college in the sense of a university college nor even a present day art-school which offers degrees for full-time students. Indeed, one of Lethaby's aims was to provide art training for 'all who are to be engaged in building in any skilled capacity'.[2]

The original school was housed in an old building in Upper Regent Street, London, and from the beginning there was a strong feeling of enthusiasm with many part-time, essentially amateur students. The studios were open during the day, but actual tuition was given in the evenings when classes began at seven o'clock. The atmosphere there was described by Esther Wood:

> . . . the students assemble in their various departments; each branch of study being open to men and women equally, with the exception of the life class for men. Some curious varieties of personality and character may be seen in almost every room. Young and middle aged men, strong manual labourers, refined and scholarly-looking craftsmen, quiet, earnest girls and smart little lads scarcely out of their fourth standard are gathered together round the tables and desks or think-ing out their designs plodding steadily on at some set task.[3]

When he began teaching at Central in 1898, Edward Johnston was hardly more than a self-taught enthusiast himself; nevertheless, he gave profound and careful thought to the validity of reviving the craft which, even in 1898, was tainted by antiquarianism. He rationalised it in the manner of Ruskin:

> To justify the bringing to life of a sleeping craft, it is only necessary to show that, when awakened, it will be beautiful and useful. Morris, who was a writer

[1] W. R. Lethaby 'Arts and the function of the guilds' *Quest* magazine, 1896
[2] W. R. Lethaby 'Architectural Education' *Architectural Review*, vol xvi, 1904
[3] *Architectural Review*, vol ii, 1897, p. 241

and illuminator before he was a painter, has shown us how beautiful modern illuminated writing can be and how in every case the *method* is to be sought in the old work and inspiration is to be found in nature.[1]

Whether or not 'modern illuminated writing' would have ever truly fitted the Arts and Crafts' definition of useful is open to question. But it seems certain that Edward Johnston believed that it did. In his earliest classes were the twenty-year-old Eric Gill, then a student of architecture, Noel Rooke, the wood engraver, and Graily Hewitt, a barrister who later became a professional calligrapher and illuminator. As Johnston's daughter, Priscilla, has said: 'They made a little band of explorers in unknown country. He was the leader of the expedition, but as much an explorer as the rest.'[2] They experimented with such techniques as raised and burnished gilding and quill cutting, some of which had been passed on from the earlier researches of Morris, Cockerell and Cowlishaw. No doubt they also tried recipes from the Victorian Illumination manuals which were still very much in vogue.

Johnston had already begun to discover the implications of the square-cut pen on the shaping of letters and to form his belief in the essential part that tools and materials had to play in the creation of 'The Thing'. He experimented with letters, too, analysing and developing modern forms such as his 'Uncial' and 'Half Uncial' scripts which initially formed the basis of his teaching. In 1906, with contributions from Gill and Hewitt and illustrations by Noel Rooke, Johnston's book *Writing & Illuminating, & Lettering* was published in which some of the discoveries of the 'band of explorers' were recorded; and it has remained in print ever since.

Ironically, in seeking the method 'in the old work', they may have overlooked techniques used by the professional scriveners or law-writers who still wrote with square-cut pens on parchment every working day, in offices only a stone's throw from Johnston's and Hewitt's lodgings in Grays Inn. However, in this there was some parallel with the past, for it was not *professional* scribes of the Chanceries and stationers' shops in fourteenth century Italy who had evolved the humanistic scripts we associate with the Renaissance. It was an educated and largely independent class who were free to pursue experiment for its own sake. It was just such a class (to which Johnston belonged) which fostered the Arts and Crafts Movement in prosperous, late nineteenth-century England. It was essentially to this group and their adherents, mostly amateur enthusiasts in the best sense, as well as art students, that his book was addressed.

Irene has reminded us of Johnston's belief that 'the student must grow into his own outlook', both he and his students continued to explore and their work to evolve in a modern way. In 1912 Baroness Rosencranz was able to say that:

> Judging from signs all around us, it is very safe to foretell that with increasing demand for decorated books, artists will nurture the necessary courage which will enable them to throw over traditions which, like the pure Celtic art, have

[1] *Edward Johnston*, Faber and Faber, 1959, p. 97
[2] *Ibid.*, p. 98

become dead and irrevivable and evolve new and living traditions compatible with the spirit of the age they live in.[1]

In spite of those encouraging revolutionary signs, the simplifying spirit which Edward Johnston had brought to calligraphy was by no means immediately accepted nor were its effects evenly distributed. It was not surprising that his ideas would have taken some time to counteract the influence of the energetic publishers of the many Victorian 'facsimile' books and illumination manuals. No doubt these were well represented in the library of Irene's art school in the 1920s, just as they were in the library of the art school I attended as late as 1958.

From 1921–5 Irene attended Maidstone School of Art, studying for the Drawing and Industrial Art examinations and, eventually, for her application to the Royal College of Art. The school, like others in the country, had been set up primarily as a training-ground for industrial designers. 'Calligraphy and Illumination' was an established part of the curriculum, albeit one considered as perhaps no more than a good disciplinary and formative accomplishment: indeed, there is evidence that the subject was one traditionally used by students hoping to go on to post-graduate work at the Royal College of Art as an easy option with which to impress an examining board.

In the hierarchy of the school, full-time craft students, calligraphers included, had become a semi-elite between the fine art students and the apprenticed tradesmen who attended art school once a week. Twenty years of relatively enlightened art education had not narrowed the distance between the 'fine arts' and the 'crafts', one of the chief aims of the Arts and Craft Movement. Nevertheless, drawing was a fundamental of Irene's education as for the other students at the school and even when much of her energy was spent preparing specimens of calligraphy for her application to the Royal College, she still found time to slip away in the evenings through a side door to the adjoining museum to draw. And the memory of drawing 'Old Bones', the skeleton used in the anatomy class, was one fondly recalled by Irene at the end of her life.

At Maidstone, Irene also bound books, printed textiles, tried her hand at engraving and was able to watch students who worked at other crafts such as silver-smithing, lithography and etching. They were all developing their skills of seeing and doing, working through set projects, with tuition, criticism and support from teachers, for five days a week as well as evening classes throughout the school year.

Academic requirements for entry were not stringent and it is unlikely, apart from the study of art history, that there was much emphasis on the theory of art. It was understood that three or even four years of intensive practical work were needed to produce artist-craftsmen with enough practical skill and experience to express themselves through what they made rather than what they could say about it. In common with the other student-craftsmen, Irene would have acknowledged a kinship with the apprentice carpenters described by W. Rose in *Good Neighbours*, his recollections of life in a Buckinghamshire village in the nineteenth century: their 'double ambition

---

[1] *Studio*, vol 56, 1912

was to possess a complete set of tools and to excel in the craft. They saw in an article of beauty the reflection of its maker's character. Its excellence and his were one.'

Under the tuition of Arthur Sharp, a gifted teacher, though not a specialist in calligraphy and someone trained in an earlier school of illumination, Irene's decorative work, as a student, owes much to the designs of the Victorian illuminators, amongst others Owen Jones and Henry Shaw. However, she was familiar with, and struggled to copy, Edward Johnston's early uncial and half-uncial models from *Writing & Illuminating, & Lettering*.[1]

Johnston himself appears to have abandoned, at any rate for teaching purposes, the hands that Irene had sought so laboriously to master. After resigning from the Central School of Arts and Crafts in 1912 his teaching was concentrated on the much larger and less specialised classes at the Royal College of Art and the 'foundational hand' was evolved to give students a fair working hand and a reasonable grounding in the basics of letter-form. In his own work Johnston had progressed through a fourteenth-century book hand to a 'heavy italic' which he occasionally displayed in class. Irene was shocked to find that she had a lot of unlearning to do when she went to the Royal College of Art in 1925 and she was to find, in Johnston, a penetrating critic whose own work was approaching an oriental simplicity. But the hours of pains-taking work at Maidstone had not been wasted. The models which Johnston now found himself unable to teach had, after all, been the basis of his early teaching which had helped form Gill, Hewitt and Noel Rooke and they still proved to have been a firm enough base from which Irene could begin to make further discoveries.

Irene first saw Johnston in 1925: 'He came into the large Design Room to face a waiting class of ninety-three excited new students, crowded on forms, perched on tables and even on window ledges — most of them there because attendance at his lectures was compulsory.'[2] Only a few of these students would, like Irene, have been admitted to the College on the strength of a portfolio of calligraphy submitted from a provincial art school. So although attendance was compulsory, it diminished percep-tibly as the academic year progressed; Irene referred to herself as one of those 'who stayed the course'. Raw students discovered the merits of equally distinguished teachers such as Paul Nash or William Rothenstein, or the enthusiasms of other students who included Enid Marx, Eric Ravilious, Barbara Hepworth and Henry Moore.

Some students reacted against what they undoubtedly saw as a monkish pursuit, but the drift away from Johnston's classes each year must in part reflect the greater potential for employment in other crafts and the fame available to 'fine artists'. The calligraphers' monkishness extended to their attitude towards employment, too. At a time when Nash and Rothenstein were finding their students small but important

---

[1] It is interesting to note that these early teaching hands, introduced to Germany, by Johnston's first German students were already viewed as anachronistic there by the early 1920s. Rudolf Koch had quite justifiably insisted on the need to develop independently of Johnston, and encouraged the use of the steel pen as a genuinely modern instrument; Koch looked for a calligraphy as contemporary as the art of the Expressionists, an attitude noticeably similar to that of modern scribes and illuminators.
[2] *Tributes to Edward Johnston, op. cit.*

commissions from the printing and advertising trades, Johnston was still paying lip-service to the Arts and Crafts distrust of photo-mechanical, industrial reproduction. Johnston had chosen an abstract and apparently 'pure' discipline. His work for London Transport (from which a substantial part of his income was derived) was played down, and even disparaged by him as a concession to Mammon. So that when in 1930 Irene asked him how much she should charge for her first commission (the Oxfordshire and Buckinghamshire Light Infantry Roll of Honour, 1914–19), he wrote: 'I really know nothing about the "Market Value" of such work, and can only guess at what people may be prepared to give for it from what I myself "take".' For a calligrapher to survive by producing 'useful beauty' in the twentieth century, it meant working for print. But these were not sources of income towards which Johnston was prepared to direct students.

As one of those 'who stayed the course', Irene benefited towards the end of each year from the smaller classes which gave her more access to Johnston's personal tuition. She qualified after only two years of her three-year scholarship course, and so enjoyed a 'bonus' year without any required classes. But even after a further year's teacher training course at the Royal College of Art, the only career prospect open to her rare talents was that of teaching Art to secondary-school students in a northern industrial town. So she chose marriage, to a cousin, instead.

Though Irene later came to regret the choice of husband, marriage at least gave her 'time to think'; and at Edinburgh School of Art, where she eventually did teach (among her students there were Tom Gourdie and George Thomson), she was able to mix with other artists again and was free to develop at arm's length from Johnston, though she continued to demand of herself the exacting standards he had set.

Distance did have its problems, however, and she has told me that during that time she suffered the acute double embarrassment of having a piece of work rejected by the Society of Scribes and Illuminators' Exhibition Committee and having to explain its precipitate return to the client from whom she had specially borrowed it!

She had several commissions, but it was those things she did for their own sake which reveal most strongly her developing ability to express *emotion* in her work. The 'Journal', spontaneous broadsheets written for the staff-room notice board at the College as a gesture of support for colleagues fire-watching in the war-time night, and the deeply personal gifts made as expressions of love are near perfect pieces of workmanship.

It is not only the technical brilliance of her work but Irene's choice of texts for her manuscripts, and the nature and quality of her response to them which are of special relevance to the modern calligrapher. The stretching of the image of words in relation to the calligrapher's perception of their meaning was recently the subject of a discussion between a poet and a calligrapher. The poet Sarah Lawson complained about calligraphers 'messing about' with her words for their own purposes: 'plain type' would be better than that. It transpired, though, that she was unaware of the many different styles, design options and textures offered by 'plain type'. She was unfamiliar with the idea that calligraphy could be compared to the voice of an actor who emphasises, prolongs or otherwise 'messes around' with the words of a poem. The discussion ended for me with a remark from someone who suggested that perhaps the ideal medium for communicating poetry was Braille! But it is a discussion that might well be renewed after we have *read* Irene's manuscripts and learned to appreciate the marvellous interplay of text with image of which she was a master.

After leaving Edinburgh at the end of the war, Irene taught at Central School and in the late 1950s her calligraphy students (we still called ourselves scribes) experienced, perhaps more vividly than she had, anxieties of finding a job as college days ended. Trained as we were in the techniques of cutting quills, preparing vellum and gilding precious manuscripts, we were faced with the problem of reconciling Johnstonian ideals with the requirements of a modern world, where even our fellow art students thought that what we did was inappropriate and monkish. In 1958, most other subjects had links with the 'trade' side of their craft and work periods were arranged in industrial establishments, a textile factory or pottery for instance, as part of a student's course. It is significant that no such opportunity existed for calligraphers. There was no industry apart from commercial art studios and even there in the late 1950s hand lettering was being discarded in favour of type.

Irene was aware of our situation and our anxieties. She later told me that in her last two years of teaching at Central School she had begun a lettering class with the words 'Edward Johnston said' only to realise for the first time that such a preface held no meaning for them and that teaching without his help, so to speak, had therefore less meaning for her. It had less meaning for the colleges, too: by the early sixties most of the art schools in Britain, including Central School, also acknowledged the mood of the time by dropping courses in writing, illuminating and lettering as a specialist subject at degree level. But those of us who had 'stayed the course' as Irene's last students had been fortunate to acquire craft techniques, skills of looking and doing which had been revived and continuously extended over the decades since Johnston began teaching. We were able to imbibe something of the integrity of our own teacher Irene Wellington, whose standards would forever represent a measure for our own work. By chance we were just far enough removed in time from Johnston to be able to admire the spirit and form of his work without feeling tempted to copy his 'style'. His words: 'Within the limits of the craft we cannot have too much freedom' would indeed have described my feelings then, but what direction to take was less clear.

Exhibitions of contemporary work have always been infrequent and their audience geographically limited. It is not until recently that students have been able to study books of examples of modern calligraphy. Aside from palaeographical handbooks on historical manuscripts and Alfred Fairbank's *A Handwriting Manual* and *A Book of Scripts*, Edward Johnston's *Writing & Illuminating, & Lettering* was the only title on the list of books recommended by Irene to her classes in the late 1950s. Johnston's book we were still to regard as 'The Scribe's Bible'. Such books as we did see had as great an influence on us as those few available to Irene in her student days. *Lettering of Today*, published in 1937, was the first book to display a cross-section of contemporary work. The first edition showed us pages from Irene's *Twenty-six Days (The Journal of a Holiday)*, and in *Modern Lettering and Calligraphy* (1954) we saw recent work from the Royal College of Art, from America and from Europe and had our first glimpse of Irene's 'Violet' piece (illustrated on page 82).

Irene believed that the 'only true way to work is to make your own discoveries'. We may well have been fortunate that there were so few contemporary sources. Like Johnston and Irene before us, we were taught to look at historical examples and to go through the process of forging new designs inspired by their past excellence. Had we been able to skim off ideas from the surface of more recent experiments we may have produced something which had a semblance of modernity but would have been less well prepared to make our 'own discoveries'. Nevertheless, it was often quite easy to identify the source from which we students had lifted the beginning, at least, of many of 'our ideas'.

Modern Lettering and Calligraphy gave us strong hints, too, that there were other things to calligraphy than illuminated addresses: change was in the air. Even though comparatively few students graduated there was still little outlet for our work, whether as artist-calligraphers or lettering designers, nor was there much prospect of a job in teaching. The art schools which encouraged other crafts to develop new directions in the 1960s had almost entirely discarded 'scribing and illuminating' as irrelevant calligraphic knitting. But if Johnstonianism had failed to establish for 'modern illuminated writing' a useful role in industry or acknowledgement as an art, neither had the ideals of Koch been fully realised in the colleges of Europe and America.

In the United States during the late sixties, calligraphy teachers whose outlook perhaps owed more to German strands of the Arts and Crafts Movement which had always been more responsive to the demands of the advertising and printing industries were also being asked to close down their courses. Yet in 1973, what proved to be the first of over a hundred new American Calligraphy Societies was constituted in Los Angeles and Irene was able to anticipate 'the liveliest possibilities for an invigorating renewal'; she wrote that 'Today the teacher finds a provocative range of tools and materials which, rightly and imaginatively used in the strange climate and mood of our time could bring fresh life into the design of letter forms and play their part in creating them.' She was speaking of handwriting, but the 'strange mood and climate of our time' had produced in a comparatively affluent America a readiness to see calligraphy as an expressive and interpretive art. Largely unaware of the beliefs of Johnston or the polemics of Ruskin, Morris or Lethaby, and disdaining the class distinctions between the fine arts and calligraphy with which we had grown up, they were willing to paint with words (which is what I think Edward Johnston and Irene Wellington were doing all along).[1]

---

[1] When John Farleigh put the point to Irene that 'It would seem to be dangerously easy to adopt a visual approach to writing and think of it merely as a lovely page, forgetting legibility', Irene replied: 'Johnston did so himself — as a master may — every now and again on a book jacket or a border

It was the 'painting' in Irene's and her students' work which elicited the strongest response from those who formed the American calligraphy societies as 'self help' groups in the 1970s and early eighties. In many ways they were not unlike the amateur enthusiasts of the old Central School days, or the founders of the Society of Scribes and Illuminators when the right spirit counted for more than skill. The new vitality came from the students not the colleges: students whose enthusiasm has made them willing to devote hours and years to the study and practice of calligraphy simply because they wanted to; and having seen 'how beautiful modern illuminated writing can be', have breathed fresh life into a craft still struggling for an identity in the post-Johnston era by aiming at beauty of expression for its own sake and letting usefulness take care of itself.

Throughout her training and her working life Irene struggled to reconcile the disciplines exerted by the demandingly high craft standards and strictly held beliefs of her teacher with a strong urge towards freedom of expression and joyous decoration for its own sake. Such training was appropriate to her time and needs, but she also undoubtedly felt its constraints irksome and an unwonted check on her creative impulse. Yet her work was at its best when discipline and freedom came closest together, her skill lending enormous authority to the freedom of each mark she made.

Whereas Irene had to shed conscious technique and intellectual constraints in order to achieve freedom, the last quarter of this century has seen new generations of calligraphy students who have discovered for themselves the *need* for discipline and skill. By experiencing first the pleasures and then the limitations of freedom unaided by technical mastery, they have been led to seek its aid in order to create that beauty of expression which can only be achieved by the marriage of hand and idea.

When asked what writing meant to her personally, Irene answered: 'Writing is just a germ that has got into me, and I shouldn't be happy if I didn't do it. I can't help it.' The future of calligraphy depends on a like need within us and will reflect whatever time and space we occupy. Our marks will, if they possess life at all, speak for us and for our time: as do the examples of Irene's work in this book. Although there is in every piece something which can speak of and for her, it is those things she did purely for herself or friends, which speak most clearly and truthfully for the artist within her. It is the life and soul of Irene Wellington's work, not the belief in useful beauty, that is accepted and valued now by a much greater audience than ever before.

The example of Irene Wellington's work is inspiring more and more people to make 'living letters', as an endeavour valuable for its own sake: in Johnston's words – 'that men themselves may have more life'. It is by the nature and the quality of the love and life she was able to invest in her letters that she would want to be judged.

DONALD JACKSON

or sometimes on a broadsheet. One can easily forget legibility, and that is the danger of producing wall panels, though one may occasionally treat them quite frankly as sheer pieces of masterly decoration.' Quoted in *The Creative Craftsman* by John Farleigh (Bell & Sons Ltd, 1950), p. 119.

IRENE WELLINGTON

AN APPROACH TO HER WORK

It is very unusual for an almost complete record of someone's working life to remain intact. Generally, pieces get thrown away and papers get lost. We are fortunate indeed that Irene had a particular habit of treasuring things. She threw out very few of her working notes and rough drafts (or anything else unless necessity dictated – Hubert Wellington's name for her, 'Squirrel', was indeed apt!).

The collection of work she left behind, now mostly held at the Crafts Study Centre, Bath, is uniquely important from many points of view. Firstly, there is her historical context. She stands in direct line between Edward Johnston's pioneer work in the craft and the more personally expressive calligraphy of the present day. Secondly, writing was her medium. She was a scribe through and through; not only in the mastery of her many and various manuscript hands, but in the way she put her thoughts down. The act of putting pen to paper seemed to clarify for her the thinking process. Lastly, there is the extraordinary quantity and quality of the work itself. During her life she fulfilled the whole range of her talent, in writing, in drawing, in her approach to the craft and in the inspiration she left behind for others.

Irene's roots lay in Edward Johnston's teaching. She deeply absorbed his attitudes and standards. She said, 'To think of Johnston is to think of Truth; it was, I believe, his unswerving insistence on truth that made his teaching so alive and so deeply fixed in those who stayed the course.' She built on this foundation; and through her own search for the truth of the thing, she gradually came to realise the possibilities latent in the craft in a way that no one else had before. In her working life she stretched the whole concept of calligraphy from the formal roots of Johnston's teaching (itself embedded in historical tradition) to the freedom of personal expression.

In his maturity, Johnston emphasised paring down to absolute simplicities. Irene had great difficulty with this, as her whole personality tended towards complexity. Whereas Johnston was more interested in the structure and execution of the letter-forms themselves, Irene loved words. She enjoyed reading and choosing the texts to write out, and came to see how calligraphy could bring her visual and literary worlds together. Through the arrangement of words and drawings, and by subtle changes of colour, weight and style of letters, she found she could create a mood which reflected her own inner thoughts and feelings about the words. Also, the creative activity of writing allows for spontaneous emotional expression – an on-the-spot, spur-of-the-moment response to mark-making – which she found challenging and satisfying.

Calligraphy is a sensitive and complex art, and Irene, as a sensitive and complex person, was perfect for it as it was perfect for her. Eventually she managed to reconcile Johnston's views on truth and simplicity with her own complicated imaginative qualities, and to see how a proliferation of ideas could be contained within a unifying order and structure. In doing so, she evolved her own special language, which she continued to develop throughout her life.

Her formal pieces are classic, with an absolute rightness of scale and dignity appropriate to the occasion. They always bear, in writing and in drawing, that liveliness of touch which is her special hallmark. However ceremonial these pieces are, they usually include some reference or detail that is personal to her. Some of these come out of extensive research. For The Bailiffs of Lydd panel, she read up a vast amount of background information on the Cinque Ports, as she wanted to include something of their history in the bottom area of the design. In the end she used only a fraction of the material gathered. At other times the appropriate quotation would spring from the wealth of her general reading. An example of this is the incorporation of two William Dunbar poems in the Queen's Accession Address, commissioned by the London County Council in 1952. One poem was 'In praise of the City of London'; the other, 'In praise of a Lady', likened her to a Lily and a Rose. Both are nicely judged compliments. Her touch is subtle: there for the readers to find for themselves.

But it is in the work she did for herself and as presents for her friends, where there were no restrictions, or requirements to be fulfilled, that Irene is at her best. The right choice of words, written with great freedom and enjoyment, and embellished with all kinds of decoration – both beautiful and witty – all go to make up something that is uniquely her own.

Her output was vast, though spasmodic, reflecting the ups and downs of her life. Sometimes she would finish a most complicated piece of work 'in a matter of three days, directly at great speed . . . to encourage students to complete an idea quickly before it dies, so as to see how "the thing made" can as a *whole* carry their, or its, faults acceptably' (Czech Christmas Carol, 1948). At other times, she worked on roughs again and again, exploring every facet until she was satisfied. This perhaps reveals something of her personality. Imagination often walks hand-in-hand with indecision: there is always another alternative, another way of looking at things, yet another possibility. But she had also a keen intellect and a devastating honesty. These she used to cut through all her conflicting ideas to find the kernel of truth in the end; though this process was at excruciating cost to herself. She had the capacity to let go and allow something to come up out of the darkness as well as the ability to focus the searchlight. These two elements maybe reflected her essential belief in God and the pursuit of Truth which were so central to her character and attitudes.

All craftsmen are of their period. They cannot escape it. Their value is finally measured by whether or not their work survives their era. As soon as a work of art is completed, it begins to die. It only lives again in the hearts and minds and imaginations of those people who look at it; in the meaning and significance it has for them.

There has to be some element beyond fashion that subsequent generations can find there for themselves. One element is a kind of inner vitality that comes from a marriage of supreme (and often hard-won) craftsmanship and a deep personal search. It comes through all the confines of the craft, through all the selection and rejection of traditional sources and contemporary influences, towards something that is *real* for that person. Therefore it is born new and fresh and living and vital at that precise moment of making. And if it is truly alive then, it can be reborn at any time. Irene's work has that quality.

ANN HECHLE

IRENE WELLINGTON
AS A TEACHER

Irene Wellington began teaching in 1932 at the Edinburgh College of Art. She later taught at the RCA and for some years at the Central School in London. Although she said she enjoyed teaching, she found it took a lot out of her – but she continued to do it because she believed in it, and that it was her contribution to the continuance of calligraphy and its traditions. It was at the Central School in 1958 that I had the good fortune to be able to study under Irene in what were to be her last two years of teaching. I can really only write of my time with her then.

She came in one day a week. We were very lucky as there were only about ten students in the class, and only three of us specializing in calligraphy. She preferred to give individual tuition rather than class demonstrations or lectures, although she did give a few of these. A one-to-one situation more readily suited her approach. Like Edward Johnston, after a certain amount of initial instruction, and practice of manu-script hands, she wanted 'Real Things', as only in doing them would the subtleties of the subject become apparent. She used to devise special projects for each person. These projects were nicely judged according to the student's experience and ability and tuned to their personality and interests. (She had train note-books in which she jotted down ideas during the journey to and from Henley: suggestions for a panel on the subject of the seasons for one student perhaps, a book of poetry for another, a reproduction of a Persian manuscript for a third.) I remember as a very young and raw student being half fascinated and half appalled at the complexity of some of the ideas she would bring for us to work on.

Her approach to the work, I think, was the key to why she was so different from anyone else. She went straight to the heart of the matter. 'What is your intention?' she would ask, and by encouraging you to explain to her what you meant, you clarified it also to yourself. And she built on that; she had that extraordinary ability to take the whole thing apart, reveal the underlying truth about it, and re-shape it in a way you knew to be right. Of course, in doing so she uncovered all your muddled ideas, woolly thinking and pretensions. (She had the most wonderful eye for a fraud – if you'd cooked up something the night before, she knew. You couldn't hide from her.)

It all sounds very frightening, as indeed it was. Her criticism was devastating. Because your work was you, you were on the line. But she was never destructive. Her criticism, though uncomfortable, left you feeling, not bereft, but somehow uncluttered. You sen-sed the larger perception, and even if you couldn't bring your idea off, you felt you had firmer ground to stand on, and a further vision to stretch for.

It is difficult now to look back twenty/five years and remember what being her student felt like then: to separate it from the interpretations of hindsight. I do remember being deeply frustrated by her perfectionism. Nothing was ever quite right (and it wasn't!), because what you really wanted to do as a student (I am speaking for myself here!) was to play safe, work within your capacity and build up a nice fat portfolio for your end/of/term show. But Irene wasn't interested in something looking good. She wanted it to *be* good (the looking good would perhaps come later). She wasn't interested in the quick and easy answers, the ones which are concerned with the hand/ling of design and writing only. She wanted you to get to the truth of the thing. Two things she said of Edward Johnston are also, I think, true of her: the search for the Truth, and the insistence on absolute pitch.

Irene said herself that she would rather have you flounder and struggle a bit than let it appear too easy, because then you became more aware of the subtleties and possibili/ties of the subject. She made you feel that you were always stretching beyond your capacity – and *now* I think that perhaps she was, too. There was that element of risk, of living dangerously. She let your design grow out of the intention of the work itself in a way that was also new to her. She never covered herself by falling back on the tried and tested designs and conventions that she herself had worked through, and knew would work, and thereby pushing your idea into a ready/made slot. Context was all. The work was always a unique thing in its own right. It had to be *real*, and real to you.

It sounds as though it was a very intellectual approach – always analysing: 'What does it mean?' But somehow it wasn't. She always allowed for the intuitive, irrational element that can't be explained. The element which says 'I want it pink'; and she would let you have it pink. She would never interfere with that. But that intuitive spark for most of us only illuminates part of the whole; the rest has to be sorted out by hard work.

Those who teach know how difficult it is. It is one thing to give free and exciting projects, as she did, but to cope with all the half formulated and wild ideas that come back is quite another. To channel those ideas without crippling them, and to awaken others to their own potential, shows a teacher of quite remarkable calibre. Irene asked questions, she suggested, she showed, she brought things to read and to look at. She never forced. She let it come from you.

I remember she wrote on a postcard before our final exam the advice of Oliver Cromwell to his troops: 'Trust in God, and keep your powder dry'! Her characteristic humour, with a nice blend of the spiritual and the practical thrown in.

It didn't suit everyone – this slow and difficult way. Some people feel happier with more direct guidance; but of course we all want to 'be taught' rather than 'to learn'. But what she was doing was tuning *you*. The conventional rules will serve for a number of things as there are optimum relationships and standard answers that will work. But they don't allow for growth and change. They don't hold good in all contexts, and you can't stretch them to encompass a new kind of vision. The only real tuning fork is you. Irene instinctively knew this. She let you discover for yourself.

All her personal characteristics went into her teaching: her humour, her compassion, her integrity and her commitment to the craft and to you, the student. Looking back, I don't think she decided that was how she was going to teach. Quite simply, that is how she *was*.

ANN HECHLE

CRAFTSMANSHIP

TOOLS AND MATERIALS

Irene Wellington's attitude towards technique is encapsulated in the lines from W. B. Yeats that she would quote when asked about the training of art students in calligraphy:

> A line will take us hours maybe;
> Yet if it does not seem a moment's thought
> Our stitching and unstitching has been nought.

Her manuscript notes 'Some Reasons and "Findings"' (illustrated pages 46 and 47) show the immense care she took with materials. On the preparation of vellum she specifically identifies the three essential qualities looked for by Edward Johnston in good writing, namely, freedom, sharpness, and unity:

> The proper preparation of the skin helps to give all these qualities. The right matt surface gives sharpness . . . prevents uneven colour or black, (unity) . . . certainly helps freedom as it gives just enough resistance for the pen not to slip or skate, & this control gives freedom.

The only way to avoid what she describes as 'a scribe's nightmare – a greasy surface, a blunt pen and a glutinous ink so that the pen lifts only in thick, lumpy strokes'[1] was constantly to recut the pen and to prepare the vellum properly, regarding it as much a tool as the pen. She knew that craft skills and techniques had to be mastered if she was to narrow the gap between her ideas, her inspiration and the reality of the created thing. Skills thus prepared become a bridge between our spiritual and temporal worlds, but not always easily.

For normal writing, Irene worked at a board held up at an angle of 45°; when writing with colour she had the board almost flat:

> Colours are thicker and coarser than ink and do not flow down the pen so well: they need the extra angle that a flat board gives the pen. One is of course freer and the writing is more lively if one can have the board at a fairly steep angle.[2]

As the illustrations in this book show, the amount of preparation or 'rehearsal' time before committing herself to a finished piece of work was by modern standards

[1] 'Quoted in *The Creative Craftsman* by John Farleigh (Bell & Sons Ltd, 1950), p. 127
[2] *Ibid.*, p. 127

(ABOVE) Irene at work

(OVERLEAF)
THE PREPARATION OF VELLUM
White House *c.* 1950

Brown and blue-black ink, green ballpoint on lined paper.
23 × 18 cm (each sheet)

enormous. She made pages of tracings so as to capture the optimum shapes and textures of the many tiny elements which were eventually assembled to create her sensitively orchestrated designs. Once these 'finished roughs' were completed, paper or vellum would be prepared and a faint framework of lines as a guide for the work was ruled in pencil or scored with a fine polished agate point.

She would select pens from the strong flight feathers of a swan, turkey, goose or crow and then shape and trim to suit the different sizes of writing to be used. When a quill became blunt, she preferred to resharpen it and risk a slight variation in nib-width rather than pick up another which, though sharp, may have felt strange to the hand

THE PREPARATION OF VELLUM.

WHY ?   a) for sharpness.
b) For opaque solidity of ink and colour

The three essential qualities that Edward Johnston looked for
in good writing :—
I   Sharpness.
II Unity
iii Freedom.

The proper preparation of skin helps to give all these qualities.
I   The right "matt" surface gives sharpness.
II "   "   "   " prevents uneven colour or black (unity).
III "   "   "   " certainly helps freedom as it gives just
enough resistance for pen not to slip or skate & this control gives freedom.

THE PUMICE POWDER (OR POUNCE).
Removes grease & gives "matt" surface.

THE GUM SANDARAC
makes the ink blacker
gives sharper edges as it prevents the ink or colour spreading.

WHAT SURFACE do you want?
Non greasy & } pen flattens the pile & makes trough in
slightly velvety } which ink and colour can remain.

HOW to get this required surface
FIRST judge the nature of the skin's surface by holding
it up sideways to the light.
Then USE. Finest glass paper or sometimes coarser 'garnet' paper
{ this stretched round a block of wood. }

Preparation of the
HAIR SIDE of SKIN { this is best & most sympathetic }   * rub.
Shatter on plenty of pumice powder, pounce* this with the
covered block for 5 — 10 – 15 — 20 minutes, or even longer † rarely
quite vigorously. Dust off with old piece of silk.

NEXT

Shatter a little dusting of powdered gum sandarac,
rub this in with the same block — clean off with silk
It is easy to get too much gum on this side.

FLESH-SIDE of skin.

Treat this in the same way, but tentatively, watching carefully
how it reacts { if a good skin it can be done nearly as much
as on the other side }.
If it reacts badly & drags up the surface or the veins, stop at once,
If any fear of a bad skin "pumice" or rub it very little & do so
with cartridge paper only on the block instead of glass paper
using pumice powder merely to remove the grease
Put distinctly more sandarac on the flesh side than on the
                                                      hair side.

WARNINGS.

i   Be careful to have no little grits of gum or dirt or even a crumb
    of india-rubber under any sheets being prepared, or a hole may be rubbed

ii To go on rubbing too long or with too little pounce (or pumice powder)
    may simply POLISH the surface.

iii Do not put too much gum sandarac on as the ink then springs away
    from the middle of the letters (touching up destroys the directness
    of the writing }. It is difficult to remove the gum from a matt surface
    whereas more can be added, if needed, even after work is begun.

iv Do not sacrifice a good surface just because you are tempted
    to retain a pleasant colour of skin.

v. In the finest thin skins { New Zealand or Norwegian) sand paper ^(glass)
    is not needed — is too harsh a treatment only pumice with
    paper round block or with a rag only. On the delicate, light weight skins

* this side is   BEWARE* of flesh-side — prepare as little as possible, but use
sometimes
treacherously   perhaps an exceptional amount of sandarac.
porous.

ERASURES. I do mine on hair side with a very sharp knife tentatively
    working both ways, never in one direction only.
    On the flesh-side questionable to erase at all. frankly cross out (or scratch
    (possible sometimes on a good skin, judgement can be used,   not scratch
    The surface RARELY but sometimes is improved on a thick skin if good)

Green "ink Rubber"? some people use.   Never use ordinary India rubber on skin
              I PREFER KNIFE.

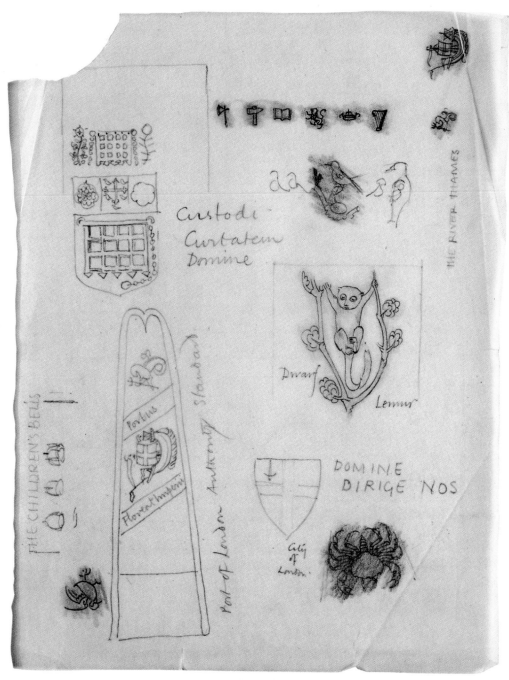

The River Thames

Custodi
Curtatem
Domine

Dwarf

Lemur

The Children's Bells

Portus

Floreat Imperium

Port of London Authority Standard

DOMINE
DIRIGE NOS

City
of
London.

TOWER OF LONDON
Edinburgh 1936–7

Pencil, tracing paper.
25.5 × 19 cm

Each tiny element of a complex design was first drawn and transferred to tracing paper. The various heraldic components would then be positioned and re-positioned within a shield to achieve a happy disposition of space around the positive image of each motif. In spite of the time spent on arranging details and rehearsing their shape, the finished piece would be completed at a speed which would make the whole seem freshly conceived and spontaneously executed.

When Love on Earth set up his rest
    Within a safe and secret place,
h is stronghold was a Virgin's breast,
    h is light her stooping face.
        Then oped the everlasting bars
        Then sky-bells rung,
        And all the lovers of the stars
        Came down and s ✛ u ✛ N ✛ g ✛

For since Love may not dwell alone,
    Around h im, in attendant train,
Those flaming fires which were his throne
    Fell down to earth like rain.
        O happy, happy falling FIRES,
        That from your height
        I nto a world of blind desires
        Bring GIFT of SIGHT!

the WORD goes FORTH: and round him drawn,
    h ark, in unending voice of song,
The birds of God's immortal dawn,
    S ing, to sing out man's wrong.
        O happy, happy birds of night!
        That from your rest
        Stoop down, and from the fields of light
        Make earth your nest.

Around the stable shone that light,
    Within the stall that song was heard,
But showed not there as stars to sight,
    N or sang like voice of bird.
        The sound — a Maiden's heaving heart,
        All full of GRACE
        The light, of heaven's dawn a part,
        her stooping face!

Laurence Housman

When Love on Earth set up his rest
    Within a safe and secret place,
h is stronghold was a Virgin's breast,
    h is light her stooping face.
        Then oped the everlasting bars
        Then sky-bells rung,
        And all the lovers of the stars
        Came down and s ✛ u ✛ N ✛ g ✛

WHEN LOVE ON EARTH
Edinburgh 1940

Vellum, black ink, red and blue watercolour.
14 × 18 cm (open)

Irene seldom rejoiced in skill for its own sake, but this Christmas Carol is a tour de force of technical dexterity. The carefully prepared surface of the limp parchment sustains the fine hairlines of the tiny letters written with a sharply cut quill. Almost invisible to the naked eye in the original size, the exquisite detail of this simple masterpiece of craftsmanship can only be suggested in reproduction.

and disturbed the rhythm of the piece. In later years she used steel pens for small writing, but characteristically prepared and sharpened them with such care that it is impossible to tell with certainty what was written with a steel pen and what with a crow quill. Ink was loaded into the pen with a brush, the handle of which she used to press down onto the sometimes springy vellum to keep it flat and steady as she wrote.

Irene made black ink by grinding Chinese stick ink in a dish or ink-stone with several drops of pure water. An ink stick is a compressed cake of fine soot taken from the smoke of oil or resinous woods and bound together by water-soluble gum. Freshly ground, it produces a free-running but opaque and permanent carbon black ink perfectly suited to the sharp contrasts and spontaneity of the square-cut nib of a quill.

Coloured inks bought from the shop do not usually have the covering power or free-running qualities needed for comfortable writing, nor do they dry with an even tone. Irene prepared her own opaque colours with great care, from dry powdered pig-ments mixed with gum, and from gouache watercolours. She used powdered gold, tempered with gum and water for small details and finishings. Although powdered gold was once known by the sumptuous name of 'liquid gold', it produces a modest glimmer compared with burnished gold leaf; but it can be quickly and effectively applied with pen or brush and it imparts a 'quiet liveliness' to much of her work.

Raised gold was an important visual option in the formal design of a manuscript:

> The letter is laid down with gesso first, written with a quill with an extra long split, the gesso being just fluid enough to flow from the pen without clogging. This produces a raised letter which should not be too high in relief or it will look rather vulgar. The purpose of the gesso is to lay a ground for the gold, something on which the gold can be burnished. The slight relief of the gesso gives the gold a variety of tone; the light catches the raised portion of the form according to the angle of the light, which gives an interesting sparkle to the page. This glitter is dependant on the position of light, which, since it varies, must be an unknown factor. As the page of a book curves, the gold reflects the light at different moments – sometimes brilliant, sometimes looking almost black. Because of this effect letters and forms in gold need to be made broader than they would be in black or colour.[1]

The technique of raised and burnished gilding, using a gesso base made from pow-dered white lead, plaster, sugar and fish glue, was always a problem for her. When gilding the Winchester Roll of Honour she had to make eight attempts before she was satisfied with it, 'sometimes getting up at five in the morning in order to catch the right conditions of light, humidity, etc., to enable the gold to stick satisfactorily'.[2]

[1] Quoted in *The Creative Craftsman* by John Farleigh (Bell & Sons Ltd, 1950), p. 127
[2] *Ibid.*, p. 127

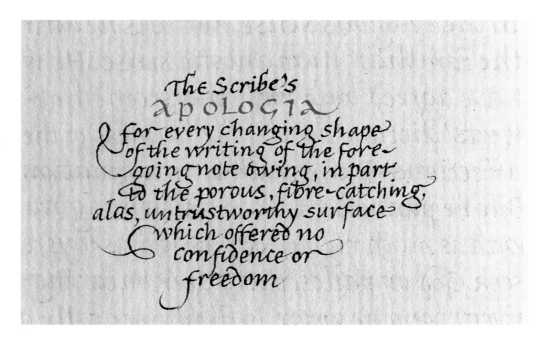

THE SCRIBE'S APOLOGIA
White House

From a book, Peter Quince at the Clavier, written on Bodleian paper; black ink, red watercolour paint.
3 × 5 cm (text size)

Irene liked the colour and surface appearance of the Bodleian paper, but it did not repay her most careful efforts. She therefore added this 'scribe's apologia'. In the note she emphasises the frustration which results when the three elements – ink, pen and surface – are not working in harmony. Confidence and thus freedom are lost.

Of course, Irene made the usual mistakes of spelling, missed words, or even made the occasional blot. Usually a misspelling would be honestly acknowledged in the Johnstonian manner by a frank correction. If circumstances favoured, a blot might find itself turned into a bird! On the question of erasures, she would have agreed with Qadi Ahmad, the seventeenth-century Persian scribe who wrote 'Do not make corrections with a pen knife. Scribes are not surgeons.' But doubtless she permitted herself a second thought from time to time and vellum or good paper will forgive the occasional attentions of a deftly applied scalpel.

In spite of her sensitive concern for the integrity of her tools and the behaviour of her materials, she confessed to enjoying only very rarely a sense of actual mastery over the tools; and indeed felt it dangerous if she did. Certain papers defeated even her best efforts, as the explanatory colophon written at the front of a small manuscript book (*illustrated above*) shows. For Irene, technique and skill were directed to just that end: the achievement of confidence and freedom which would enable her to capture in tangible form, with as much life and truth as she could, the images provided by the generous inspiration of her spirit.

DONALD JACKSON

THE ART OF
IRENE WELLINGTON

It was Irene Wellington's wish that as many of the drawings, manuscripts, and writings which she produced during her lifetime and were still in her possession, together with work by other calligraphers which she owned, should be made freely available for exhibition and study by students and those interested in writing, illuminating and lettering for the future benefit of the craft. In addition Irene Wellington hoped that other examples of her work presently in private collections could be acquired and made available for study in this way.

To this end, it was decided that the main body of such works should be entrusted to the Crafts Study Centre, Holburne Museum, Bath and a smaller but representative collection of her manuscripts should be available for study and display in the United States at the Minnesota Manuscript Initiative, The University of Minnesota, Minneapolis. Study facilities are also available at the Holburne Museum, Bath, but by appointment only.

The captions for *The Defence of Guenevere* and *Idylls of the King* by Alfred Lord Tennyson (pages 56–8 and 61) have been written by Donald Jackson. I discussed most of the captions for the other works illustrated with both him and Heather Collins.

Note: In the dimensions of Irene Wellington's work, the height is given before the width.

ANN HECHLE

IRENE WELLINGTON, *c.* 1974

(RIGHT)
TOURNEY HALL: etching
RCA 1929

Print made from a copper etching
plate.
7.5 × 7.5 cm

The house where Irene was born.
It belonged to her parents: their
names can be seen etched in the
border. She was the youngest of
nine children, five boys and four
girls; here they are lined up on
either side of the house. The
house and favourite farm animals
(see Eustace the bull, top right)
provided a source of inspiration to
which she returned again and
again.

(CENTRE)
FATHER'S WRITING 1873
(BELOW RIGHT)
MOTHER'S WRITING
c. 1880

The letter from her father, writing
home from school at the age of 13,
and her mother's less fluent exam
piece (written with a pointed steel
pen in a copper-plate script) show
the importance attached to
penmanship in the school
curriculum of the previous
generation.

54

A recurring theme, starting in the
early days on the farm at Lydd,
that ran right through Irene's life
was her interest in horses. She was
captivated by their grace.

Irene with her sister Rose.

THE DEFENCE OF GUENEVERE
Maidstone School of Art 1925

Illuminated double opening on parchment; raised and burnished gold; black ink, watercolour paint.
30.5 × 46 cm

The half-uncial and versal capitals used in Irene's student work at Maidstone show how much she was influenced by Johnston's book of 1906, but the decoration is a curious blend of motifs culled from the Victorian illumination manuals which had begun to appear in the mid-1800s and of Pre-Raphaelite influences no doubt passed on by her teacher Arthur Sharp.

The urge to decorate and to conjure with many different elements in the same design contrast strongly with Johnston's own approach. By 1925, when Irene became his student at the Royal College of Art, he had discarded the half-uncial script, which Irene was copying here, in favour of other modernised hands.

BUT knowing
now that they

   would have her speak
She threw her wet hair backward
     from her brow
Her hand close to her mouth touch-
     ing her cheek

As though she had had there a
     shameful blow
And feeling it shameful to feel aught
     but shame
All through her heart, yet felt her
     cheek burned so

Detail of horseman

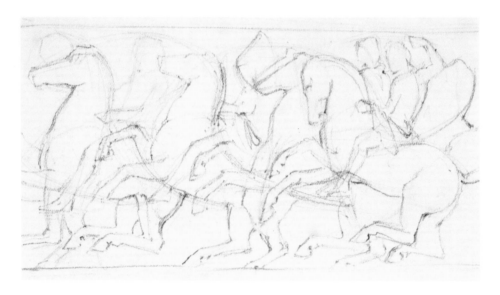

HORSEMEN: Museum study
Maidstone School of Art or RCA *c.* 1921–30

Pencil drawing on paper.

Such accomplishment in drawing (see The Defence of Guenevere) only
comes from many hours of practice and observation.

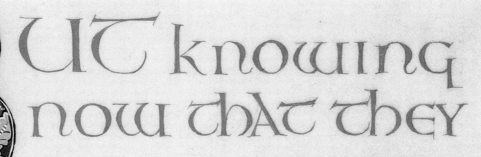

BUT knowing
now that they
would have her speak
She threw her wet hair backward
from her brow
her hand close to her mouth touching her cheek

Detail of writing

Clearly, Irene was influenced by Edward Johnston's model for a 'Modernized Half-Uncial'
in his book, *Writing & Illuminating, & Lettering*, first published in 1906.

abcdefghijklm
nopqrstuvxyz:

Modernized Half-Uncial (I.).

WRITING & ILLUMINATING, & LETTERING by Edward Johnston 1906

Detail from page 71 of published book.

In his earlier teachings, Johnston thought this manuscript hand an excellent model to start
from, as it best revealed the thick and thin strokes made by a broad-edged pen. Later he
revised this idea, as he thought it looked too archaic, and advocated a tenth-century hand
as a starting point.

O GOD THE FATHER OF HEAVEN

have mercy upon us
miserable sinners

O God the father of
heaven have mercy upon
us miserable sinners

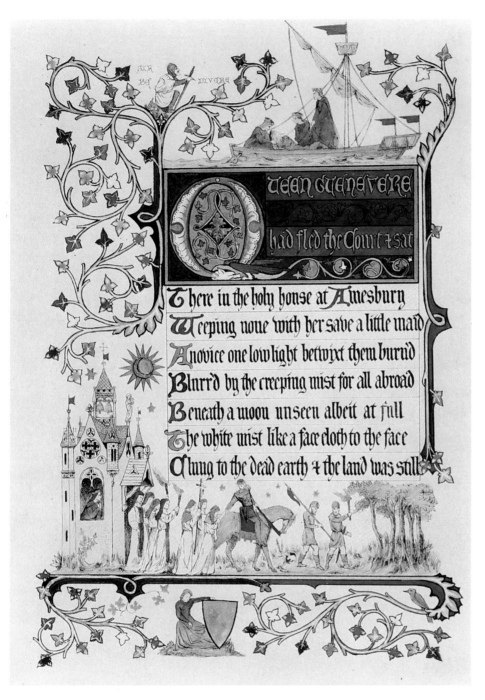

Lithographed text and outline
published in 1862.

The nineteenth-century taste for
antiquarianism was reflected in
the number of 'facsimile'
publications based on mediaeval
manuscripts and Victorian
'illuminated' gift books printed
by the then newly developed
multi-colour process of
chromolithography. They must
have helped to create a sizeable
amateur interest in writing texts
and illuminating them because
this example, published by the art
material supplier Windsor and
Newton in 1862, has a printed
text with outline drawings meant
to be hand-coloured by the
purchaser.

The nineteenth-century gothic
letter-shapes were first carefully
drawn in outline with a finely
pointed pen and then filled in.

The consistency of weight,
rhythm and form which would
have come more naturally from
the direct use of a broad-edged
pen has been lost. It was to
Edward Johnston's great credit
that though largely self-taught he
soon perceived the fundamental
weakness of 'crow-quill gothic'
and developed true pen-forms for
himself and his students.

However, the early work of
Johnston and of Irene Wellington
over twenty years later show that
they were both strongly
influenced by the work of
Victorian illuminators.
Johnston's own work ultimately
developed an almost oriental
simplicity, but the medium of the
decorated page never lost its
attraction for Irene Wellington:
countless designs on various
themes produced over the years
attest to her enduring fascination
with the problem of combining
writing with decoration.

(OPPOSITE)
THE LITANY
Maidstone School of Art 1925

Book bound in dark blue hide; parchment, raised and burnished gold, black ink,
watercolour paint.
33 × 25 cm

The scale and shape of the leaves and flowers in the border of The Litany echo the style
of Graily Hewitt and other members of the newly formed Society of Scribes and Illuminators
which held its inaugural exhibition while Irene was a student at Maidstone.

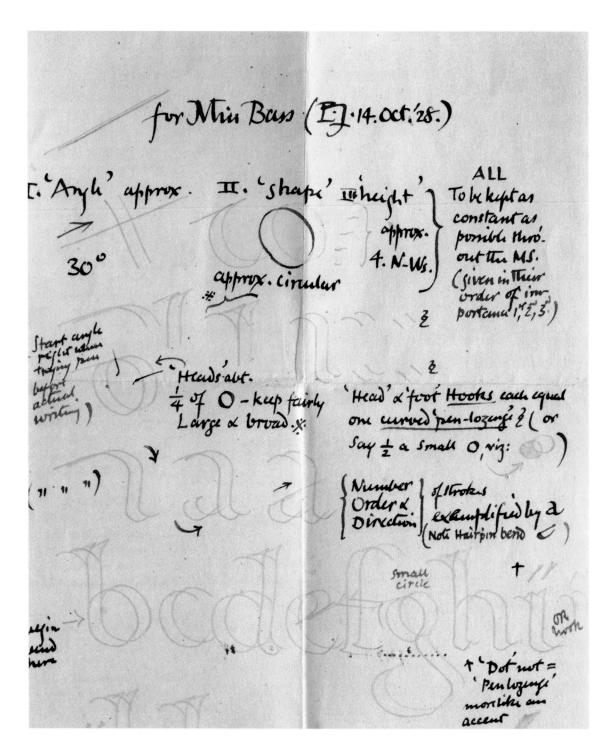

EXEMPLAR: written out for Irene by Edward Johnston (*detail*)
RCA 1928

Pen, ink and pencil on paper.
33 × 17.5 cm

Irene's first year at the RCA was a time of uncertainty. She had come to the College with
an outdated attitude to writing, and had to struggle to revise the manuscript hands that
she had been using at Maidstone and which were based on Johnston's book of 1906 (his
thinking of twenty years earlier). Under his guidance, she had to rebuild her whole
understanding of letter forms.

62

prone to boggle; a chap
with a tendency to take
every path but the proper

one, with a sidelong tact
for the alleys.
he bolts!
he's off! evasit, erupit!
'Oh,' exclaimed the man
dashing his hand a ⌁
gainst his knee head, ⁊
lifting his knee in an a-

Double opening

(ABOVE) *Frontispiece* (ABOVE RIGHT) *Detail of page*

ON THE GRACES AND ANXIETIES OF
PIG-DRIVING
RCA *c.* 1927

Book, bound in red leather; red and blue watercolour
on vellum/parchment.
16 × 12 cm (*closed*)

The writing follows Johnston's teaching of his
'Foundational Hand' which was based on an English
Caroline minuscule written in Winchester in the
tenth century. Irene's execution of it is still rather
unsure, though the drawings are much more
confidently handled, and seem to capture effortlessly
the spirit of the late 1920s. Johnston advocated
drawing with a broad-edged pen to create a greater
harmony between the drawing and the writing.

63

BIRDS AND BEASTS:
Museum study
Maidstone School of Art or
RCA *c.* 1921–30

Watercolour and pencil on paper.
38 × 28 cm

This sheet comes from an inch-thick folio of drawings done both at Maidstone School of Art and at the RCA.

This (together with the following examples, pages 65–9) show the all-round study required in a full-time art-school training. Drawing was seen as the primary discipline in developing the perception of space and form, and the coordination of hand and eye. Sensitive use of a variety of tools and materials was also encouraged. Subjects such as bookbinding, printmaking, etching, embroidery, and textile printing were included in the curriculum. All that is learned in each subject is carried over into other media. Thus, each stroke of the pen is informed by the artist's total experience.

MARE AND FOAL
RCA 1929

Pencil drawing on paper.
12 × 14.5 cm

Note the sensitive drawing and the feeling of contact between the mare and her foal. The foal is seen again in other pieces of Irene's work, e.g. Alphabetical Fragments (pages 120–21) and the Diary (pages 72–5). The Diary recalls counting the foals seen on the journey from Edinburgh to Lydd.

MARE AND FOAL
RCA 1929

Etching print on paper.
12 × 14.5 cm

A careful drawing has been made. This has been traced onto a copper plate which has been covered with a wax ground. An etching needle is used to scratch through the wax, following the lines of the drawing. The plate is then immersed in acid, which eats into the copper only where the needle has removed the wax. All the wax is then removed, ink is rolled onto the plate, and a print taken.

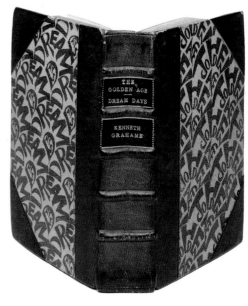

(ABOVE)
CARAVAN AND
HORSES: Drawing for an
embroidery (*detail*)
RCA *c.* 1925–30

Pencil on paper.
35 × 67 cm (*whole panel*)

(RIGHT)
IN PRAISE OF CHIMNEY
SWEEPERS: Embroidery
(*detail*)
RCA 1928

Leather- and cloth-bound book,
with partly embroidered front
cover.
24 × 15 cm (*cover*)

THIS PAGE (ABOVE AND BELOW)
PRINTS ON JAPANESE
PAPER: Lino-cuts
RCA *c.* 1925–30

Powder paint on Japanese paper.
5 × 5 cm (*block*)

Only one printing block has been
used, but the finished designs are
made from different
juxtapositions of the one block.

(OPPOSITE: BELOW RIGHT)
THE GOLDEN AGE AND
DREAM DAYS: Bookbinding
RCA *c.* 1925–30

Printed book, rebound partly in
leather, but also using prints
made from lino blocks, which
decoratively repeat the title.
18 × 12 cm (*closed*)

By craftmen and mean men, these pageants are played, and ... -ably before? better men and finer heads now come. What can be said?

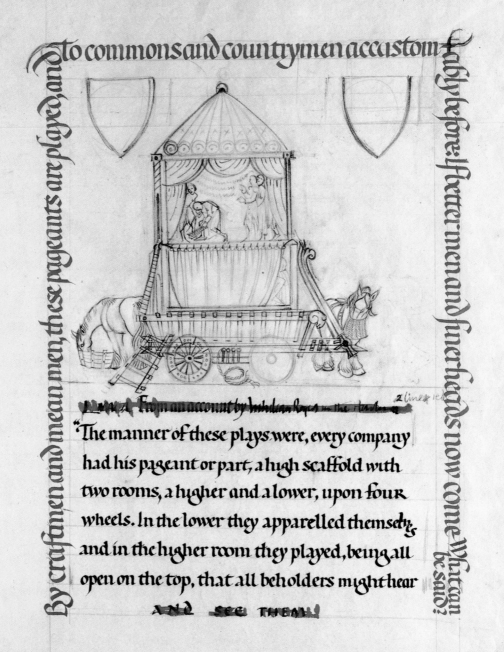

~~From an account by~~ 2 lines

"The manner of these plays were, every company had his pageant or part, a high scaffold with two rooms, a higher and a lower, upon four wheels. In the lower they apparelled themselves, and in the higher room they played, being all open on the top, that all beholders might hear

AND SEE THEM!

THE CHESTER
PAGEANT
OF THE WATER
LEADERS AND THE
WATERDRAWERS
OF ᛋ THE ᛢDEE
CONCERNING
NOAH'S
DELVGE

(OPPOSITE)
THE DELUGE: Chester
Pageant Miracle Play
RCA *c.* 1925–30

Rough: pencil, black ink and red paint on
paper.
49 × 34.5 cm

An ambitious art-school project, done at the RCA. This page was one of several for an intended book. Changes in trial drafts can be indicated very roughly (often using a brush) to give a general impression of an alternative colour or weight. The red brush marks here show that Irene was not satisfied with the simplicity of the original idea. Note also the problems of fitting a text into a tight frame. Some lines are too short, others too long (see lines 3 and 4). Irene has attempted to resolve this difficulty by changing the form of the R, and extending it; she has also squeezed in the letters of the line below. We do not know what her final solution would have been.

(LEFT)
Lino-print

Ink on paper.
53 × 33 cm

Print of lino-cut.

BUGLERS

George James Pettey	28·IV·17	Alfred James Oxlade	9·VI·15
William Ewart Carter	5·XII·16	John William Porter	14·IX·15
Levi Alexander Evetts	13·XI·16	William Charles Ridgway	30·V·15
Christopher William Fell	10·III·17	Cyril Rogers	23·VII·16
Frederick Walter Fessey	22·VIII·17	Thomas Simms	20·VII·16
Albert Fuller	13·XI·14	Stephen William Smith	9·VI·15
George Green	23·VII·16	Charles William Stanford	3·V·17
William Edward Green	21·X·14	Arthur Heath Taylor	31·XII·16
Frederick George Harper	28·IX·15	Harry Tredwell	3·VIII·16
William Howe	16·VIII·17	Frederick Willoughby Varney	2·X·18
Arthur Robert Howland	20·IV·17	Ernest John Ward	12·I·16
Rupert Lunnon	26·X·14	Frederick Wells	30·X·14
Bertram Mead	16·VIII·17	Oliver Wilkins	16·VIII·17

OXFORDSHIRE AND
BUCKINGHAMSHIRE
LIGHT INFANTRY ROLL
OF HONOUR
1914–19
Edinburgh 1930–31

Bound book on vellum; black
ink, watercolours, raised and
burnished gold.
50 × 36 cm (*single page*)

Irene's first major commission. It
took about a year to complete.
She said later that the sustained
act of writing week after week
(about 6,000 names in all) gave
her a new kind of confidence in
her writing. The sheer discipline
of continuity was a form of
apprenticeship which she valued.
The writing and planning is
heavily influenced by Edward
Johnston (particularly the double
pen-stroke capitals seen in his
Keighley Roll of Honour) and
the illuminated title page reflects
the work Irene did at Maidstone
(The Defence of Guenevere,
pages 56–9).

Alfred James Oxlade   9·VI·15
John William Porter   14·IX·15
William Charles Ridgway   30·V·15

THIS PAGE (ABOVE) *Single page* (BELOW) *Detail of writing (enlarged)*
(OPPOSITE) *Frontispiece*

DIARY: 26 DAYS
AND 25 NIGHTS OF
SUMMER (*details*)
Edinburgh 1934

Dark brown leather binding, 77
written pages; page 5 folds out.
Black ink and red paint on paper.
30 × 24.5 cm (*closed*)

The diary is of a holiday taken by
Irene and Jack Sutton from
Edinburgh to the south of
England. It was inspired by – but
not about – their honeymoon.
She made notes when they were
away, and then wrote out the
diary whilst her husband was
away for three weeks, as a surprise
for him.

Fold-out page
Complexity within simplicity: a
classic theme. On analysis, the
design is simply four panels, each
complete within itself, yet
counterpointed against the others.
Note the horizontal eyeline that
holds the central plane.
Each panel rewards closer
looking. In the first, the intervals
of verse contrast with the single
poem, and are nicely interspersed
with drawings (see also the foal
page 65). The second and fourth
panels play with different
textures. In the third, the design
revolves round a circle, and the
four winds – each with writing as
its hair! – hold the corners.
Within an apparently
symmetrical plan there are subtle
differences, and the eye is
intrigued into finding them (e.g.
the four texts which return the
circle to a square). There are also
points of rest, and therefore of
focus: Tourney Hall, which was
the holiday's destination, is at the
top, and the car they travelled in
– with its red wheels, so
important in the design – is at the
bottom.

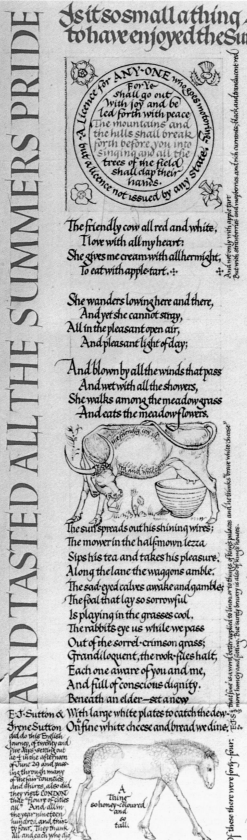

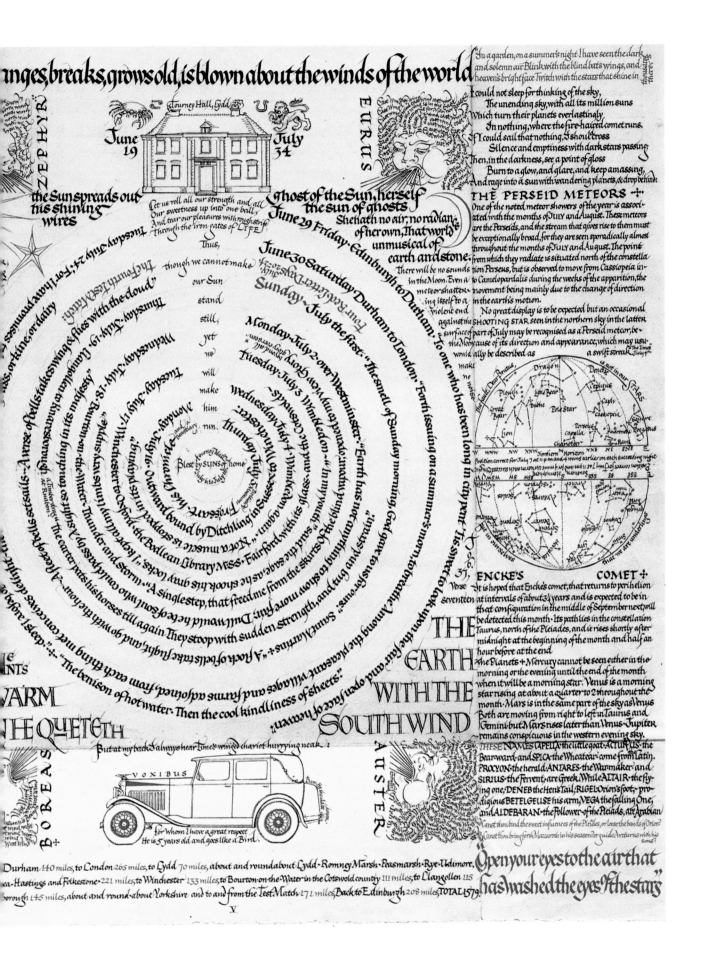

nges, breaks, grows old, is blown about the winds of the world

ZEPHYR

EURUS

June 19

Journey Hall, Lydd

July 34

the sun spreads out his shining wires

ghost of the Sun, herself the sun of ghosts

June 29 Friday · Edinburgh to Durham

Let us roll all our strength and all
Our sweetness up into one ball,
And tear our pleasures with rough strife
Through the iron gates of LIFE

Thus,

She hath no air, no radiance of her own, that world unmusical of earth and stone.

though we cannot make our Sun stand still, yet we will make him run.

Blest by SUNS of home

June 30 Saturday · Durham to London · "Forth issuing on a summer's morn to breathe

Sunday · July the first · "The smell of Sunday morning, God gave to us

Monday, July 2 · over Westminster · "Earth has not anything to show more fair:

Tuesday July 3 · Wimbledon · "In many youthful"

Wednesday July 4 · Thanked

Thursday July

THE EARTH WITH THE SOUTH WIND

BOREAS

AUSTER

VOXIBUS

for whom I have a great respect
He is 5 years old and goes like a Bird.

But at my back I always hear Time's winged chariot hurrying near:

In a garden, on a summer's night I have seen the dark
and solemn air Blink with the blind bat's wings, and
heaven's bright face Twitch with the stars that shine in

I could not sleep for thinking of the sky,
The unending sky, with all its million suns
Which turn their planets everlastingly
In nothing, where the fire-haired comet runs,
If I could sail that nothing, I should trace
Silence and emptiness with dark stars passing;
Then, in the darkness, see a point of gloss
Burn to a glow, and glare, and keep amassing,
And rage into a sun with wandering planets, & drop behind

THE PERSEID METEORS

One of the noted meteor showers of the year is associated with the months of JULY and AUGUST. These meteors are the Perseids, and the stream that gives rise to them must be exceptionally broad, for they are seen sporadically almost throughout the months of July and August. The point from which they radiate is situated north of the constellation Perseus, but is observed to move from Cassiopeia in to Camelopardalis during the weeks of the apparition, the movement being mainly due to the change of direction in the earth's motion.

No great display is to be expected but an occasional SHOOTING STAR seen in the northern sky in the latter part of July may be recognised as a Perseid meteor; because of its direction and appearance, which may usually be described as a swift streak.

ENCKE'S COMET

It is hoped that Encke's comet, that returns to perihelion at intervals of about 3⅓ years and is expected to be in that configuration in the middle of September next, will be detected this month. Its path lies in the constellation Taurus, north of the Pleiades, and it rises shortly after midnight at the beginning of the month and half an hour before at the end.

The Planets · Mercury cannot be seen either in the morning or the evening until the end of the month when it will be a morning star. Venus is a morning star rising at about a quarter to 2 throughout the month. Mars is in the same part of the sky as Venus. Both are moving from right to left in Taurus and Gemini but Mars rises later than Venus. Jupiter remains conspicuous in the western evening sky.

THESE NAMES · CAPELLA the little goat · ARCTURUS the Bear-ward · and SPICA the Wheatear · come from Latin. PROCYON the herald · ANTARES the Warmaker · and SIRIUS the fervent · are Greek. While ALTAIR the flying one, DENEB the Hen's Tail, RIGEL Orion's foot, prodigious BETELGEUSE his arm, VEGA the falling One, and ALDEBARAN the Follower of the Pleiades, are Arabian

Canst thou bind the sweet influences of the Pleiades, or loose the bands of Orion?
Canst thou bring forth Mazzaroth in his season? or guide Arcturus with his sons?

"Open your eyes to the air that has washed the eyes of the stars"

Durham 140 miles, to London 265 miles, to Lydd 70 miles, about and roundabout Lydd · Romney Marsh · Peasmarsh · Rye · Udimore, Hastings and Folkestone 221 miles, to Winchester 133 miles, to Bourton-on-the-Water in the Cotswold country 111 miles, to Llangollen 115 borough 145 miles, about and round about Yorkshire and to and from the Test Match 171 miles, Back to Edinburgh 208 miles, TOTAL 1579.

Bradman's comet trailing the sky of the Australian Innings

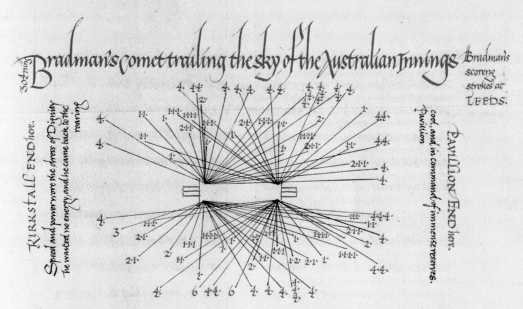

Bradman's scoring strokes at LEEDS.

KIRKSTALL END here.
Speed and power were the dress of Dignity he wasted no energy, and he came back to the maying

PAVILION END here.
cool, and in command of immense reserves. Pavilion

JULY 21st.
× Saturday

Slept so soundly & then woke to a promising morning. Bought a *Times'* and a *Manchester Guardian* before breakfast. It is fun seeing how other people record those things you have seen, and odd points that you have noticed, or have not noticed, and also seeing whether their criticism is the same as your own would be

or how it differs. We watched the kitten and puss attacking and tumbling and rolling over one another in the garden during breakfast. We then bought things "for to eat" and were away by 9.45. taking the same road in. We passed our brown foal lying as flat as foals can - and they can. We walked from the garage to the ground turning right at the

Brown foal already seen on our way in yesterday

66

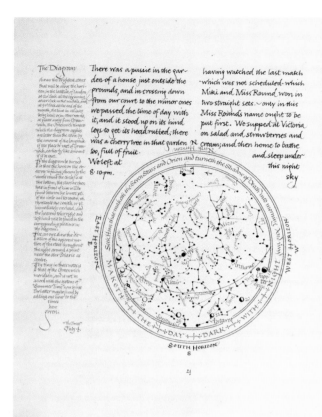

Not only is this an account of a holiday, but also an exploration of writing a book in visual terms. There are experiments with different margins and line spacing, column widths and marginal notes.

These run through the whole book.

The colophon states 'I am conscious that it should, and perhaps could, have been better written in tongue and as calligraphy, but fine writing, like graciousness, is a thing to be sought after, and only comes with striving, and withal, not too much of that.'

SONG OF THE CREATURES
Edinburgh *c.* 1943

Bound book on vellum; black ink, watercolours, raised and burnished gold.
19 × 26 cm (*approx*)

Away from the direct influence of Edward Johnston, Irene was developing her own characteristic approach to her work and her delight in the interpretation of words is clearly seen here. Almost every phrase has its own colour and flavour (see the flames surrounding Brother Fire). Although the basis of Johnston's teaching is apparent in the letter-forms, Irene felt free to adapt them to suit her own personal response to the words. In his maturity, Johnston emphasized paring down to absolute simplicities. Irene had great difficulty with this, as her whole personality tended towards complexity. This piece shows how Irene was beginning to reconcile these two viewpoints: to see how the design could be structured enough to contain complexity; and in doing so she was evolving her own special language, which she continued to develop throughout her life.

Detail

In the small panel of pen-drawn flowers and creatures, see how the words are woven into the pattern. The lettering and the drawing work in harmony. Each plays an equal part in the decoration.

Rough: black ink and pencil on paper (*detail*)

GIVE ME THE WINGS OF FAITH
Edinburgh 1940

Book on paper, bound in red
leather and paper. Black ink, red
and blue watercolours. Pen
illustrations.
29 × 43 cm

Written out as a wedding present
for the Revd. Donald R. Lee;
forty years later, he returned it to
Irene, so that it could join her
other work at the Crafts Study
Centre in Bath.

Irene remembered: 'I have a
distinct sense of this being good
writing, and one of the category of
things NOT
COMMISSIONED, but gifts
which always proved to belong to
my best work.'

This is an unusual balance for a
double-page spread. The
simplicity of the left-hand page
contrasts with the variety of
interest of the right. They hold
together by virtue of the overall
shape. The pen drawing is
reminiscent of the Anglo-Saxon
manuscripts.

It is always intimidating to add
(usually with a different pen) the
inset capital letters to an already
written text. The A and **C** in the
left-hand page betray a slight
unsureness of scale and execution.
This hesitancy appears awkward
in a page otherwise so confidently
handled.

"Will ye not shew me which of us is for
the king of Israel?" And one of his ser-
vants said, "None, my lord, O king: but
Elisha, the prophet that is in Israel,
telleth the king of Israel the words
that thou speakest in thy bedchamber."
And he said, "Go and spy where he
is, that I may send and fetch him."
And it was told him, saying, "Behold, he
is in Dothan."
Therefore sent he thither horses, &
chariots, & a great host: & they came
by night, & compassed the city about.

And when the servant of the man of God was risen early, and gone forth, behold, an host compassed the city both with horses and chariots. And his servant said unto him, "Alas, my master! how shall we do?" And he answered, "Fear not: for they that be with us are more than they that be with them." And Elisha prayed, and said "Lord, I pray thee, open his eyes, that he may see." And the Lord opened the eyes of the young man, that he saw: and

BEHOLD-THE MOUNTAIN WAS

FULL OF HORSES AND CHARIOTS
OF FIRE ROUND ABOUT ELISHA

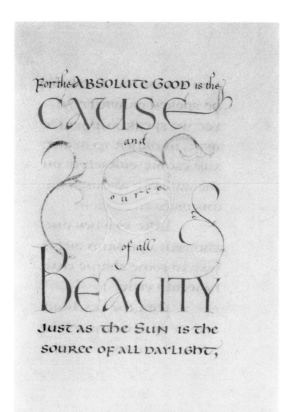

FOR THE ABSOLUTE GOOD
Edinburgh 1941

Two folds of delicate vellum, written in black ink and red and blue watercolour with quills. Raised and burnished gold S on first page.

14 × 9 cm *(closed)*

Sent to Edward Johnston for Christmas 1941. His letter of thanks (opposite) includes painstaking criticisms of the shape of the S and of the preparation of the vellum: an example of the exacting standards that Johnston expected of his students. Even though this was a gift and Irene had left the RCA eleven years previously, Johnston obviously felt he still had a responsibility to maintain his criteria of 'Absolute Pitch' and point the way to further excellence.

The pages are beautifully balanced, with a modernized uncial on the left and Foundational Hand on the right. Note the careful placing of the emphasis in red italic 'the vision itself'. Also the flow-over of the uncials on to the following page which form a heading to the rest of the text. The content and form work together: 'Strain and see' in red makes you want to turn the page.

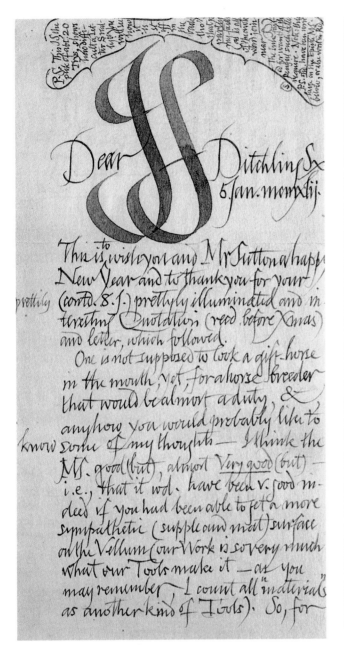
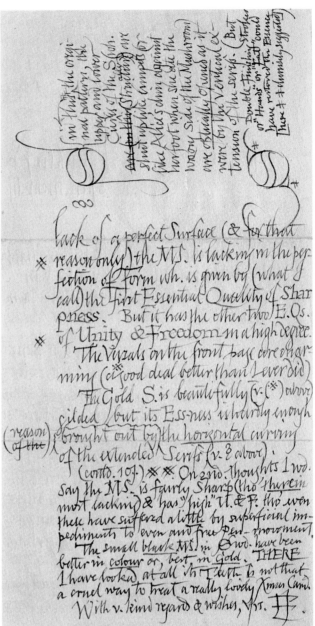

LETTER FROM EDWARD JOHNSTON
Ditchling 1942

Ink on paper
27 × 14 cm

DEEP SPRINGS OF HAPPINESS (Violet)
Edinburgh 1942

Black ink and watercolour written with a crow quill on vellum.
14 × 9 cm

Executed as a birthday present for Charlotte Wellington
(Hubert's first wife) on a fold of delicate vellum. The lines from
Robert Bridges' 'The Testament of Beauty' are written in the
shape of a leaf. Written with a crow quill, but the violet painted
with a brush. Irene said she would hesitate to suggest this mixture
of techniques to students as it was a difficult thing to bring off:
the quill pen and brush make such different strokes.
This was one of Irene's favourite pieces.

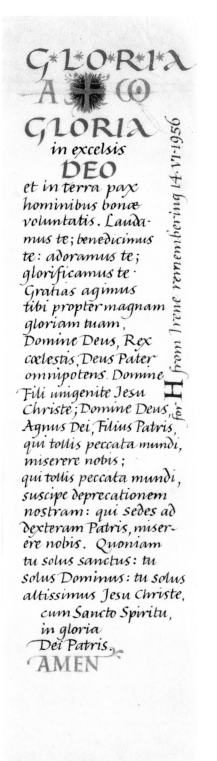

BIRTHDAY POSTCARD
Edinburgh 1943

White postcard, blue and red crayon, sealing wax.
7.5 × 12.5 cm

THAT THE TRIAL OF YOUR FAITH
Edinburgh 1942

Offcut of vellum, black ink, blue and red paint,
raised and burnished gold.
3 × 5.5 cm

Three gifts for Hubert.
It is impossible in reproduction to capture the true
vitality of the 'real thing'. These pieces, though, show
something of the special quality of intimacy, so
appropriate to the small gift, which can be expressed
in this scale.

GLORIA IN EXCELSIS DEO
The White House 1956

Paper, black ink, blue and red paint,
shell gold.
22 × 6 cm

HUBERT WELLINGTON APPRECIATION
Edinburgh 1942

Double opening on vellum, two separate panels bound in a folder of pale brown leather. Black ink, watercolour paints, raised and burnished gold. Water-stained in the centre.

38 × 29 cm (*closed*)

This was done as a Presentation to Hubert Wellington on his retirement as Principal of the Edinburgh College of Art. The piece was not commissioned, but something Irene wanted to do. In a letter to Hubert (dated 26 January 1943) Irene estimated that the work took her:

8 days of gilding @ £3	£24
A sleepless Friday night and Saturday morning to sketch it	£00
7 days to write @ £2	£14
7 days to decorate @ £2	£14
7 days drawing detail of design @ £2	£14
Cost of vellum & binding	£5
Sweat	£1
Total:	£72

In another estimate, Irene gave the cost as £64 ('would probably do it for £50 but took longer really'). It is fortunate for us that Irene did not have to live on her income as a scribe, as she always found it difficult to achieve a balance between effort and remuneration.

(CENTRE)
Detail
Incorporated with the flower is the violet from Charlotte's birthday card. The White House is seen, bottom left.

(BELOW)
Detail
Note the visual link of the angel 'giving' and the word 'given'.

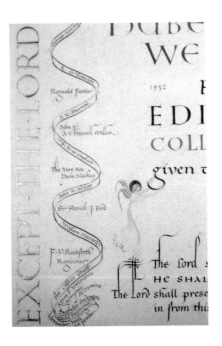

MY HEART IS LIKE A
SINGING BIRD
Edinburgh 1943

Ingres paper and coloured
pencils.
30 × 16 cm

A triptych of folded paper,
rounded at the top. The centre
panel is written and drawn over
very freely, using coloured
pencils. It was done as a birthday
card for Hubert, and includes a
singing bird and squirrel, both of
which occur in other work.
Note the 'uprush' of the whole
design. It is pinned at the bottom
where the word 'gladder' fuses
with 'love' to form the keystone of
both the meaning and the design.

the **I** leaned upon a coppice gate
darkling   When Frost was spectre-gray,
thrush   And Winter's dregs made desolate
   The weakening eye of day.
   The tangled bine-stems scored the sky
   Like strings from broken lyres,
   And all mankind that haunted nigh
   Had sought their household fires.
   The land's sharp features seemed to be
   The Century's corpse outleant;
   His crypt the cloudy canopy,
   The wind his death-lament.
   The ancient pulse of germ and birth
   Was shrunken hard and dry,
   And every spirit upon earth
   Seemed fervourless as I.

At once a voice burst forth among
   The bleak twigs overhead
In a full-hearted evensong
   Of joy unlimited;
An aged thrush, frail, gaunt and small,
   In blast-beruffled plume,
Had chosen thus to fling his soul
   Upon the growing gloom.
So little cause for carollings
   Of such ecstatic sound
Was written on terrestrial things
   Afar or nigh around,
That I could think there trembled through
   His happy good-night air
Some blessed hope whereof he knew
   And I was unaware.   Thomas Hardy

MS of   The earth lies open breasted
Benedictbeuern   In gentleness of spring,
   Who lay so close and frozen
   In winter's blustering.
   The northern winds are quiet,
   The west wind winnowing,
   In all this sweet renewing
   How shall a man not sing?
   Now go the young men singing
   And singing every bird,
   Harder is he than iron
   Whom Beauty hath not stirred.

And colder than the rocks is he
   Who is not set on fire,
When cloudless are our spirits,
   Serene and still the air.
Behold, all things are springing
   With life come from the dead.
The cold that wrought for evil
   Is routed now and fled.
The lovely earth hath brought to birth
   All flowers, all fragrancy.
Cato himself would soften
   At such sweet instancy.

MS.   Now, Winter, yieldeth all thy dreariness,
of   The cold is over, all thy frozenness,
Benedict-All frost and fog, and wind's untowardness,
-beuern All sullenness, uncomely sluggishness,
   Paleness and anger, grief and haggardness.

Comes now the spring with all her fair arrays,
Never a cloud to stain the shining days;
Sparkle at night the starry Pleiades.
Now is the time come of all graciousness,
   Now is the fairest time of gentilesse.

3-1-43

MS of The earth lies open breasted
Benedictbeuern In gentleness of spring,
Who lay so close and frozen
In winter's blustering.
The northern winds are quiet,
The west wind winnowing,
In all this sweet renewing
how shall a man not sing?
Now go the young men singing
And singing every bird,
harder is he than iron
Whom Beauty hath not stirred.

(ABOVE) *Detail*

THE DARKLING THRUSH
Edinburgh 1943

Paper, black ink, red and blue paint.
91 × 59 cm

Irene did a series of these panels for the staff-room at Edinburgh College of Art for firewatchers during the war. They were done very quickly without much planning, on cheap paper, writing with a steel pen.

Irene's early training with a quill gave her a spontaneity which she was able to carry over into the manipulation of a steel pen. Because the quill is a more flexible and sensitive instrument and it releases ink more readily than a steel pen, the strokes it makes need to be anticipated earlier, and can be maintained later; this allows for a greater 'catching in' of the white spaces. Also, the freedom of the flow of the ink makes for a discovery of speed of movement, and within that a personal rhythm.

(RIGHT)
IRENE WELLINGTON
COPYBOOKS
The White House *c.* 1955 and
1957
London 1977

Double opening from printed
book.
18 × 46 cm

Conceived as a series of
copybooks, after the manner of
the Victorian copybooks that
Irene's father and mother may
have studied. The first publisher
was James Barrie, succeeded by
Heinemann. It was originally to
be in four parts. The first three
parts were published between
1955 and 1957. Book 4 remained
incomplete for twenty years until
Louis Strick of the Pentalic
Corporation suggested that the
four parts be incorporated into
one omnibus edition, which was
then published in 1977. It is still
in print.
Irene felt that handwriting was
always an expression of the
culture of its time and deserved
more profound consideration
than was usually given in the
school curriculum.
The two pages and details
reproduced here give little
indication of the *vast* amount of
work that went into these books,
both in the selection of the
charming texts and in the actual
writing of the examples. Some
idea can be given in that the
rough trials, dummy books and
rejects fill a fair-sized suitcase!

(BELOW RIGHT)
IRENE WELLINGTON
COPYBOOKS

From the omnibus edition, back
jacket.
7 × 14 cm (*approx*)

Three grey geese in a green field grazing
g y & z   Grey were the geese & green was the grazing

Three grey geese in a green field grazing
g y & z   Grey were the geese & green was the grazin

& the ampersand

The margin & couplets above show varieties of 'tails.'

& and & and & and & and & and &

The ampersand monogram derives from the Latin 'et'

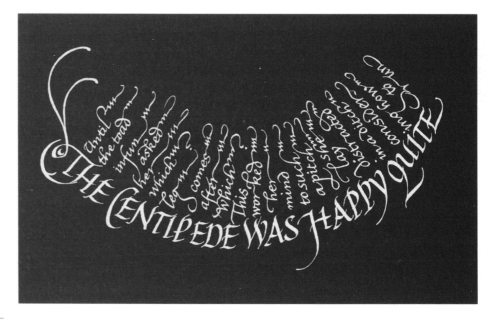

ursive" means "running"

ups of different joining strokes

cd abcd efg hij hij klm klm lmn op pq pq

tuvw xy y and az or z abcd efg efg ghi etc

ster writing involves varied joins: cultivate 'm' rhythm

r ef of; and el or el el el ol and eh or eh oh: ob ob

rf rf rh rb rf rh rf rb rl rb rh wh and qu etc

rt deft indefatigable doff repel mongrel molten

77

q The essential virtues of good lettering are readableness, b
q The essential virtues of freer faster writing g g g Ruski
steeper an angle blunter pen. flows too fast and thick? a
Much steeper this should give the faster hand.? Sir Syd
Sir Syd
Question g g Is this good enough for the really cursive I do

curator heroism damping heraldic cutting
curator heroic heraldry heraldic cutti
misdoing
mineral nautica kingly narcissus n

mineral nautical natural mislaid rot
rotund roundelay violin dough doi

Edward Johnston
Edward Johnston writes:—
The "Essential Forms"
may be defined briefly
as the necessary parts.
They constitute the skel
ton or structural plan
of an alphabet: & one
of the finest things the
letter. craftsman can do.
One of th' finest things
letter craftsman can
letter craftsman
Edward Johnston writes:—
Edward Johnston writes!—
Johnston writes:—
Edward Johnston writes:—
Edward Johnston writes:—

JUST LIKE ONE WHO WANTS TO LEARN TO WRITE (Meister Eckhart)
The White House 1948

Fold-out on paper, containing seven panels: black ink and watercolour.
16 × 87 cm

A concertina fold-out design done for Lord Cholmondeley, to whom Irene was giving lessons in calligraphy. The outside sections carry an exhortation on the approach to the work.

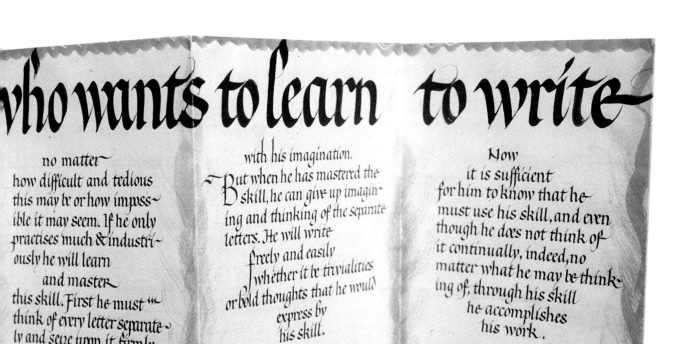

who wants to learn to write

no matter how difficult and tedious this may be or how imposs-ible it may seem. If he only practises much & industri-ously he will learn and master this skill. First he must think of every letter separate-ly and seize upon it firmly

with his imagination. But when he has mastered the skill, he can give up imagin-ing and thinking of the separate letters. He will write freely and easily whether it be trivialities or bold thoughts that he would express by his skill.

Now it is sufficient for him to know that he must use his skill, and even though he does not think of it continually, indeed, no matter what he may be think-ing of, through his skill he accomplishes his work.

B C D E F G H I J K L M N O P Q R S T U V W X Y Z

roman

I heard a linnet courting
His lady in the spring:
His mates were idly sporting,
Nor stayed to hear him sing
His song of love.—
I fear my speech distorting
His tender love.

FIRST VERSE

lateral compression

The phrases of his pleading
Were full of young delight;
And she that gave him heeding
Interpreted aright
His gay, sweet notes,—
So sadly marred in reading,—
His tender notes.

SECOND VERSE

Italic

And when he ceased, the hearer
Awaited the refrain,
Till swiftly perching nearer
He sang his song again
His pretty song:—
Would that my verse spake clearer
His tender song!

THIRD VERSE

The inside includes a series of alphabets with constructional diagrams and exemplar texts.
See how the accidental ink blot on the 'l' in 'lateral compression' has been transformed
into a bird!

THE FOUNDATIONAL HAND: exemplar
The White House 1945 and 1947

Reverse print.
40 × 27 cm

Reverse print of an exemplar panel for students. The original was written in black ink on paper, with the intention of reversing the image. The panel begins with a 'Foundational' alphabet. This is followed by the same alphabet described with a double pen, showing the order of the pen strokes and construction of letter forms.

The verses are from a sixteenth-century carol 'The Builders' and demonstrate what the letters look like, *en masse*, as 'the Real Thing'. It was an important part of Irene's way of teaching (inherited from Edward Johnston) that once the fundamental shapes of the letters had been grasped by the student (however inadequately) the only real experience of writing was to be gained by doing 'things', i.e. manuscript books, panels, etc. As Johnston said, 'Practice only teaches you to practise.' The thinking behind this was that although some guidelines have to be given in the early stages of learning, these rules are not absolute: they change in varying contexts. Only by doing 'Real Things' would the student acquire the ability to make intuitive judgements about the relationships of letterforms with each other and to the whole design, and eventually develop a sense of rightness in each unique setting. The footnote was added two years later in 1947.

CZECH CHRISTMAS CAROL
The White House 1948

Reverse print.
31 × 38 cm

The original was written on hand-made paper in black ink, with the intention of reversing it for reproduction.

Irene wrote in a letter to a friend: 'Folding Xmas card – versals are poor, not really for universal publication, but one gets used to weaknesses. Executed at red hot speed. It was personal then. It was for my students as a Christmas joie de vivre. Folded once laterally and then three times in the obvious uprights. Written in three days directly at great speed before Christmas for my own students to show pattern-making possibilities of texture of the line and the grouping of different kinds of letters. To encourage students to complete an idea quickly before it dies, so as to see how "the thing made" can as a *whole* carry their, or its, faults acceptably.'

(BELOW LEFT)
Card when folded
This shows a cut-out in the shape of a leaf, with the Christ child, ox and ass showing through from the inner page. The decoration and writing on the outside was not printed, but added by hand later.

(BELOW RIGHT)
Envelope
Decorated with a drawing of holly and 'A Merry Christmas' written with a music pen.

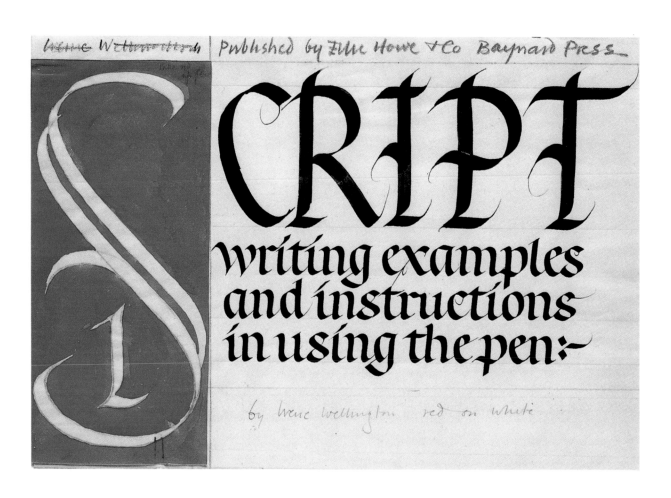

SCRIPT
writing examples
and instructions
in using the pen:-

by Irene Wellington   red on white

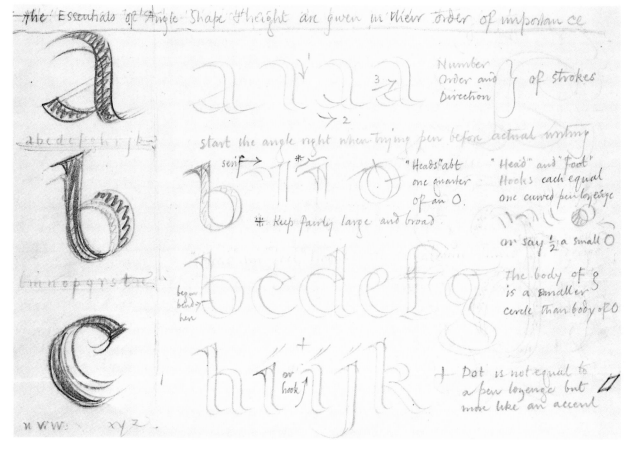

The Essentials of Angle Shape & height are given in their order of importance

Number Order and of strokes Direction

start the angle right when trying pen before actual writing

serif

"Heads" abt one quarter of an O.

"Head" and "Foot" Hooks each equal one curved pen lozenge

Keep fairly large and broad.

or say ½ a small O

begin bend pen hn

The body of g is a smaller circle than body of O

+ or hook

+ Dot is not equal to a pen lozenge but more like an accent

abcdefghijk
lmnopqrstu
vw xyz.

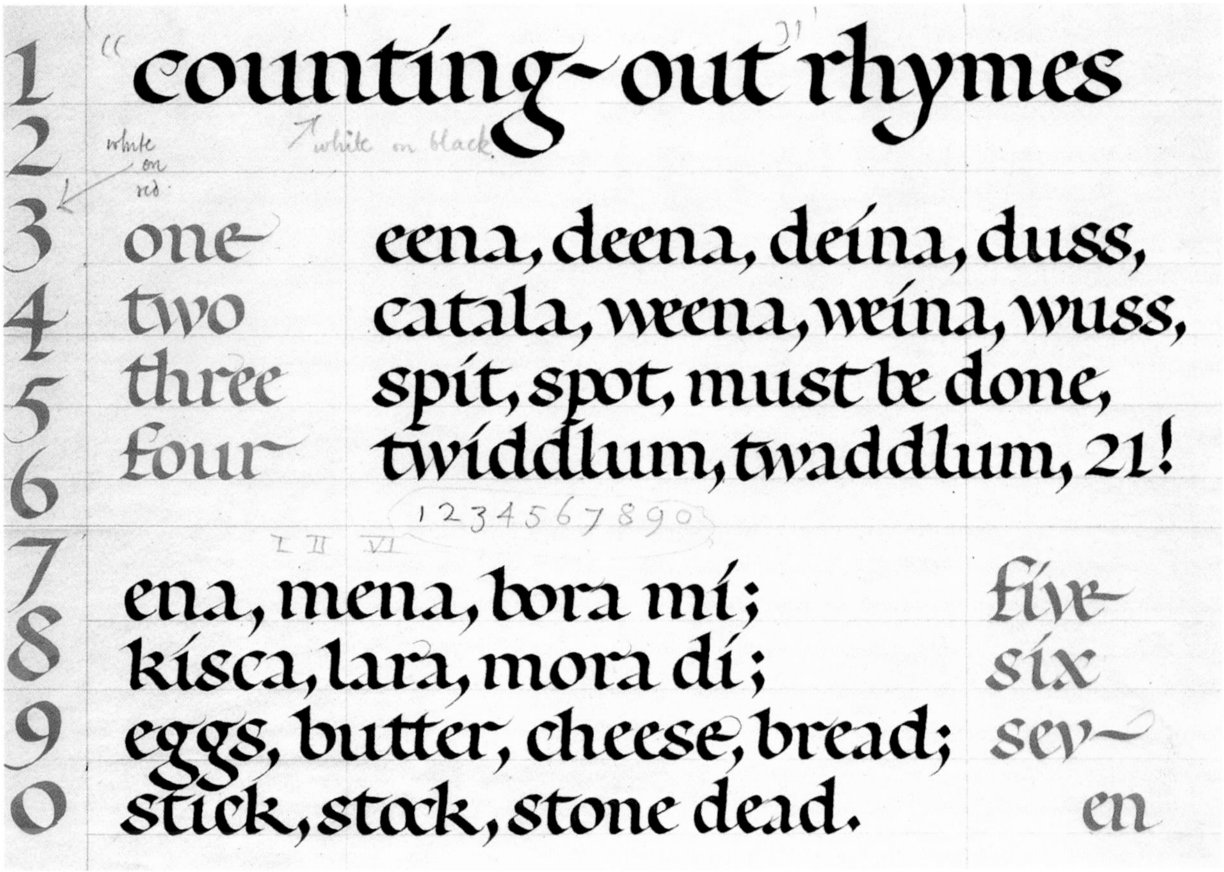

"counting~out rhymes

one   eena, deena, deina, duss,
two   catala, weena, weina, wuss,
three   spit, spot, must be done,
four   twiddlum, twaddlum, 21!

1234567890

ena, mena, bora mi;   five
kisca, lara, mora di;   six
eggs, butter, cheese, bread;   sev~
stick, stock, stone dead.   en

SCRIPT (Ellic Howe book)
The White House *c.* 1944–60

Roughs for an intended book. Black ink, red paint and pencil on paper.

Irene struggled unsuccessfully for years to write a book on the fundamentals of calligraphy. Although it appears to be well on its way to publication, it was abandoned. It is not known why. Irene felt such a responsibility to convey the subtleties of the subject that perhaps she found it difficult to encompass her ideas in a book.

Writing an instructional book is in direct conflict with the process of teaching itself. All teaching is a kind of exploration, for the teacher as well as the student. Ideas are constantly changing and evolving. To write a book, then, is like stopping a film, freezing the action to a single frame. To fix on any one thing in this moving sequence, knowing it will be isolated out of its proper context, and that it may assume a didactic importance never originally intended, is a daunting notion.

upon being given a

1 firstly give thanks

The holly & the ivy
When they are both
full grown.
Of all the trees
that are in
the wood
The holly
bears
the
crown

'THE
HOLLY'

The holly
bears a
blossom
As white as the
lily flower
And Mary bore
sweet JESUS CHRIST
TO BE OUR Sweet SAViOUR

& THE
IVY

SYBIL norf

TO ROCK

19

2 secondly admire it's

AND THE
RUNNING

The holly bears
a berry
As red as
any blood
And
Mary
bore
sweet
Jesus
Christ
To
do
poor
sinners
good

OF
THE
DEER

is the
back-
ground
CAR-
OL

beauty

3 preserve it's

wing

UPON BEING GIVEN A NORFOLK TURKEY FOR CHRISTMAS
The White House 1950

Double opening on Bodleian paper, bound in Cockerell combed paper, with red leather
spine. Chinese ink and watercolour.
39 × 24.5 cm

Irene wrote in a personal note: 'Own text and background carol of "The Holly and the
Ivy"; purely personal spontaneous gift to the Marquess and Marchioness of Cholmondeley.
Exhibited in London (?date) and Maidstone 1964. Sheer play. Designed and executed
within the spare time of three days. . . . Cursive italic free for the background carol. The

96

heavy text? A compressed easy hand, not Gothic, not italic, not quite a compressed "Foundational", too easy in the arches for that as I remember.'

A deceptively simple arrangement, balanced but not strictly symmetrical. On first glance the two pages seem to mirror each other (e.g. the ribbons that form the mantling of the crest), but on closer looking there are differences, and the eye is intrigued into finding them.

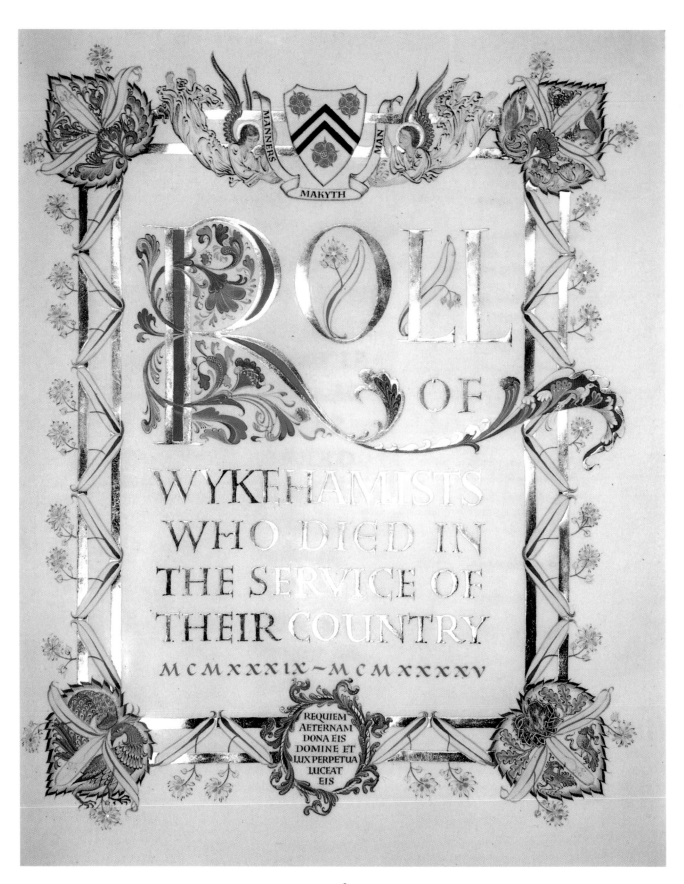

MANNERS MAKYTH MAN

ROLL OF
WYKEHAMISTS
WHO DIED IN
THE SERVICE OF
THEIR COUNTRY
MCMXXXIX ~ MCMXXXXV

REQUIEM
AETERNAM
DONA EIS
DOMINE ET
LUX PERPETUA
LUCEAT
EIS

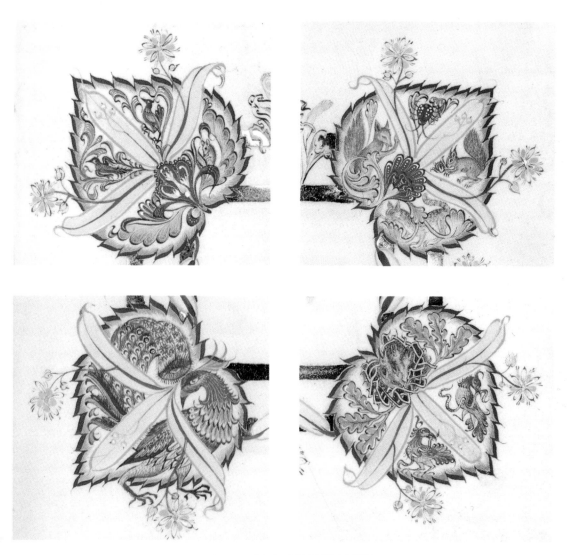

WYKEHAMIST ROLL OF HONOUR 1939–45
The White House 1948

Vellum book, bound by Roger Powell. Black ink, watercolour, raised and burnished gold.
Frontispiece.
43 × 30 cm (*single page*)

The design of the frontispiece is directly inspired by the tenth-century Winchester school of illumination. One of the traditional forms of decoration found in the manuscript books of this time is a central panel of writing or illumination, framed by a double-banded border of gold, with bosses at the corners.

Irene has based her idea on this, but instead of imitating the historical acanthus-leaf decoration of that period, she has used the motifs of the lime flower and leaf, because, as she stated in her colophon, 'Nothing so recalls Winchester to the mind and memory as the scent of limes.' The coat of arms displayed at the top is that of William of Wykeham (1367–1404), the founder of Winchester School. The angels, with their fluttering draperies, are reminiscent of Anglo-Saxon manuscripts.

99

(RIGHT)
Detail

An example of successful organization of information on a page: every separate fact has its appropriate value, yet all work in harmony. The name was considered to be of greatest importance, therefore it dominates the other details of rank, regiment, etc., but each holds its place across the page by differences of weight, colour or style of writing.

(OPPOSITE)
Rough trials

Many experimental drafts were done before the final selection was made. These changes can be seen in details of the six rough drafts shown here, but the exact sequence is not known.

To have the name written first, on the left, might appear to be the natural position for it, but a more central placing was thought to provide a better balance to the design as a whole. An italic for the name was eventually chosen in preference to a more open roman hand, as the pattern it creates is blacker and richer and makes a far greater contrast to the other writing. The alternating black and red in the last column gives a sparkle to the page, and also helps to clarify the information. The fourth was chosen.

(PAGES 102 AND 103)
Some trials and tracings

KRRC.	Lieut	Luxmoore, R.C	A 1936-41 College	Died of wounds Belgium September 16th 1944 Commines
Royal Engineers.	Major	Macdonald, A.J.	1913-18	May 27th 1940
Argyll & Sutherland Highlanders	Major	Macdonald, C.A	B 1926-31	Off Malaya March 1st 1942
8th Hussars,	Lieut	McDonnell, R.E	F 1928-33	d.o.w. after Agedabia February 16th 1941
Cameron Highlanders serving with Partisans	Captain	Mackenzie, A.D.	B 1928-33	Northern Italy October 6th 1944
Seaforth Highlanders	Lieut	Mackenzie, R.H.A	K 1934-39	Accident in Caithness May 1942
R.A.F.V.R.	Flying-Officer	Maclagan, G.	A 1930-34	Over Warnemunde May 9th 1942
R.O.S.B.	Lt-Col	Maclaren, J.D.A	A 1918-23	d.o.w. received in Burma April 20th 1944
Intelligence-Corps,	Captain	Macleod, Sir Ian Francis Norman, Bart.,	D 1935-39	Accident near Naples April 1944
Scots Guards,	Lieut	McLeod, R.C	G 1935-40	Salerno September 11th 1943
Scots Guards,	Lieut	McMurtrie, D.G.S.	I 1937-41	d.o.w. near Anzio February 1944
R.N.	Lieut	Major, M.J.H.	K 1931-35	Off Malaya December 10th 1941
1st Royal Dragoons attached Sherwood Rangers	Captain	Makins, G.E.	D 1920-32	d.o.w. received in France September 4th 1944
Hampshire Regt.	Lt-Col	Mallock, J.R.C.	B 1922-27	Normandy July 13th 1944
The Queen's Royal Regt.	Captain	Mansel, M.L	B 1931-36	d.o.w. after Kohima May 13th 1944
Scots Guards,	Lieut	Marshall, H.W.S	A 1936-41	Holland November 26th 1944
Coldstream Guards	Lieut	Martyn, D.V.	I 1937-42	Normandy August 4th 1944
Rifle Brigade,	Lieut	May, G.T.	A 1935-40	Villers Bocage June 14th 1944
Coldstream Guards,	Lieut	Meinertzhagen, D.	C 1938-42	Near Nijmegen October 2nd 1944
Green Howards,	Major	Middleditch, J.G.	E 1920-26	Died in India March 1942

100

Name	Rank	Regiment	House/Years	Place/Date
Armitage, J.L.F.	Major	Royal Artillery	Coll 1933-37	Bir El Feheim Jan 24th 1942
Ashton, C.T.	Sqdn Ldr	R.A.F.V.R	E 1915-1920	Accident over Carnarvon October 31st 1942.
Atkinson, J.E.A.	Captain	Rifle Brigade	D 1922-27	Died Sudan

Name	Rank	Regiment	Place/Date
Armitage, J.L.F	Major	H. 1917-1922 Royal Artillery. College 1933-37	Bir El Fenheim January 24th 1942
Ashton, C.T.	Sqdn Ldr	R A F V R	Accident over Carnarvon
Atkinson, J.E.A	Captain	E 1915-1920. Rifle Brigade	October 31st 1942 Died Sudan

Name	Rank	Regiment	House/Years	Place/Date
Bennett, S.B	Lieut.	R.N.V.R	E 1931-35	North Sea April 20 1942
Bird, E.A.	Lieut.	Rifle Brigade	G 1929-34	Calais May 25 1940
Burley, W.A	Lt. Col.	17/21 Lancers attached Royal Gloucestershire Hussars	G 1911-16	Knightsbridge June 1942

Regiment	Rank	Name	House/Years	Place/Date
Rifle Brigade attached Royal Gloucestershire Hussars	Lieut	Bird, E.A.	F 1937-42	Calais s May 25th 1940
17th/21st Lancers	Lieut	Birley, W.A.	H 1913-17	Knightsbridge June 1942
Rifle Brigade & Commando	Captain	Birney, D.L.	E 1936-40	St Nazaire April 28th 1942

Regiment	Rank	Name	House/Years	Place/Date
R.A.F.V.R	Sqdn Ldr	C.T. Ashton	1933-37 E	January 24th 1942 Accident over Carnarvon
Rifle Brigade	Capt.	J.E.A. Atkinson	1915-20 D	October 31st 1942 Died Sudan
		G.D. Ayre	1922-27	December 28th. 1941

Regiment	Rank	Name	House/Years	Place/Date
R.A.F.V.R	Sqdn Ldr	Ashton, C.T.	1933-37 E	January 24 1942 Accident over Carnarvon
Rifle Brigade	Capt	Atkinson, J.E.A.	1915-20 D	October 31 st 1942 Died Sudan
A.A.F	Fl. Offr	Ayre, G.D.	1922-27 G	December 28 th 1941 After Dunkirk

Assistant Master

REQUIEM
AETERNAM
DONA EIS
DOMINE ET
LUX PERPETUA
LUCEAT
EIS

CORONATION ADDRESS
The White House 1953

Vellum scroll. Capitals in red between two lines of blue writing, with the main text in black Uncials. Initial W in blue outline, decorated with red and gold. The dedication speeches on each side in brown with matt gold leaves and burnished gold.

21.5 × 35.5 cm

Irene wrote in a draft letter to Ieuan Rees to be read at a meeting of the Society of Scribes and Illuminators: 'First stirring of idea was to write the whole MS in one black hand throughout in centre flanked on either side with pale brown foliage with animals (horses) leaping through (in the manner of Eastern MSS). I felt this might have pleased the Queen but it was too lighthearted and I had to confess lack of skill to even attempt this. Essentially design included (left) Arms of LCC (presenters) and (right) Coronation Crown. Finally the uncial text was flanked on left in pale brown and gold by Elizabeth's dedicatory speech on the air from S[outh] A[frica] when she was 21, and on the right the first Christmas broadcast (now become a tradition) after her father died.'

An interestingly complementary design to the Accession Address (see page 111).

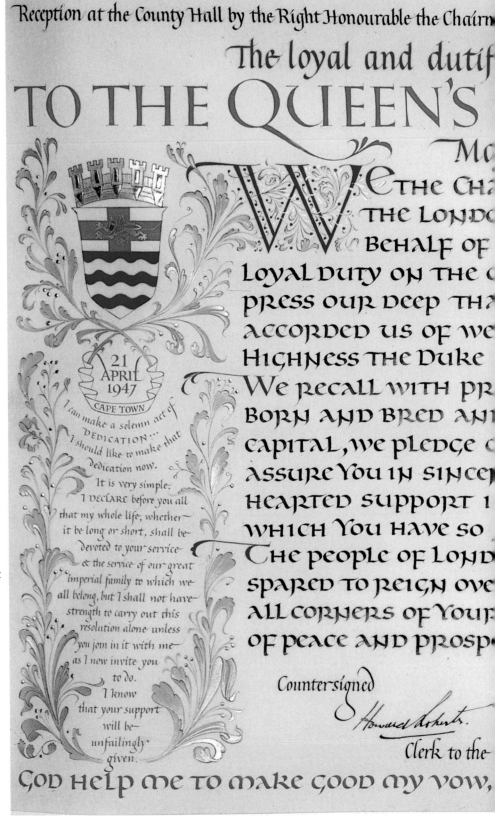

…ss of the London County Council

…ST EXCELLENT MAJESTY

…se Your Majesty:—

…ALDERMEN AND COUNCILLORS OF
…y COUNCIL, DESIRE TO OFFER, ON
…LE OF LONDON, OUR HUMBLE AND
…OF YOUR CORONATION AND TO EX-
…THE OPPORTUNITY GRACIOUSLY
…YOUR MAJESTY WITH HIS ROYAL
…URGH TO OUR COMPANY TONIGHT.
…YOUR MAJESTY IS A LONDONER
…NAME OF THE PEOPLE OF YOUR
…N DEVOTION TO YOUR SERVICE AND
…ION AND HOMAGE OF OUR WHOLE-
…SCHARGE OF THOSE HIGH DUTIES
…SUMED.
…THAT YOUR MAJESTY MAY LONG BE
…J HEALTH & HAPPINESS & THAT IN
…JWEALTH & EMPIRE THE BLESSINGS
…J EVER ATTEND YOUR REIGN.

Chairman of the Council.

…BLESS ALL OF YOU WHO ARE WILLING TO SHARE IN IT.

CHRISTMAS 1952

At my
CORONATION
next June, I shall
DEDICATE MYSELF ANEW
to your service. I shall do so in the
presence of a great congregation
drawn from every part of the
Commonwealth & Empire…
I want to ask you all…
to pray for me on that day—
to pray that God may give me
wisdom & strength
to carry out the solemn
promises I shall be making,
& that I may faithfully
serve Him & you all the
days of my life—

E R

THE BOROUGH OF LYDD
The White House 1948

Framed panel on vellum. Black ink, red and blue watercolour, raised and burnished gold.

76 × 50 cm

Irene's affection for her father and for the place of her birth found expression in this piece of work 'In oblique praise of my father'. Irene wrote at the bottom of the panel 'Charles Edward Bass. He was revered and loved by all who knew him, and by me Irene Wellington née Bass.'

Using the same hand in three different sizes, Irene has achieved contrasting densities of texture arranged in blocks, which give a three-dimensional quality. Notice how the central bold text comes to meet you, and the smaller annotations drop back. The flag-flying banner of the heading holds the whole thing in place. The management of the white spaces gives a sense of calmness and timeless dignity.

The Borough of Lydd Kent;

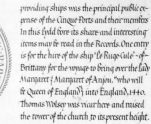

The ancient Borough of Lydd or Lyde, has been granted six Charters, the earliest in the reign of Edward the First. Lydd owes its name to the Romans who found a considerable settlement of people on the 'Littus', or Sea Shore: upon the Ripæ or Banks—now the East and West Rypes the town laid its early foundation. In Saxon times its name became 'Hlida'. Lydd is a 'limb' or member of the Cinque Port of Romney. The duty of providing ships was the principal public expense of the Cinque Ports and their members. In this Lydd bore its share and interesting items may be read in the Records. One entry is for the hire of the ship 'Le Ruge Cule' of Brittany for the voyage to bring over the Lady Margaret { Margaret of Anjou, "who will be Queen of England} into England, 1440. Thomas Wolsey was vicar here and raised the tower of the church to its present height.

Quid autem de dignitatibus

"But what shal I say of dignitees and of powers? the whiche ye men, that neither knowen verray dignitee ne verray power, areysen hem as heye as the hevene? The whiche dignitees and powers yif they comen to any wikked man, they don as grete damages and destruccions as doth the flaumbe of the mountaigne Ethna, whan the flaumbe walweth up; ne no deluge ne doth so cruel harmes.

But now, yif so be that dignitees and powers be yeven to goode men, the whiche thing is full selde, what agreable thing is ther in the dignitees or powers, but only the goodnesse of folkes that usen hem?

And therfor it is thus, that honour ne comth nat to vertu for cause of dignitee, but ayeinward honour comth to dignitee for cause of vertu." *Boethius de Philosophiæ Consolatione trans. Chaucer*

Details

107

THIS ROLL OF HONOUR

IS DEDICATED TO THE MEMORY OF
1408 OFFICERS·WARRANT·OFFICERS
NON·COMMISSIONED OFFICERS AND
MEN OF THE OXFORDSHIRE AND
BUCKINGHAMSHIRE LIGHT INFANTRY
WHO GAVE THEIR LIVES IN
THE SECOND WORLD WAR
MCMXXXIX · MCMXXXXV

Pte	Abbott, James Donald	30 Mar 1945
Pte	Ablett, John Leonard	27 May 1940
Pte	Adams, Bartholomew	10 May 1940
Pte	Adams, Edward Bernard	27 Nov 1939
Cpl	Adams, John Anthony	3 Dec 1943
Pte	Adams, Leonard	28 May 1940
Pte	Adams, Oscar Thomas	30 May 1940
Pte	Adcock, George Frederick	30 Mar 1945
Pte	Aiston, Joseph Shaw	26 May 1940
Cpl	Alderson, John Edward	1 Jan 1943
Pte	Alderson, John Frederick	

Abbott, James Donald

Ablett, John Leonard

Adams, Bartholomew

OXFORDSHIRE AND BUCKINGHAMSHIRE LIGHT INFANTRY ROLL
OF HONOUR 1939–45
The White House 1948–50

Bound book on vellum. Black ink, watercolours, raised and burnished gold.
50 × 36 cm (*single page*)

Compare this with the Oxfordshire and Buckinghamshire Light Infantry Roll of Honour
1914–19 (pages 70–1). The whole concept of the design and the writing is much more
confident and refined.

Compare these examples (*above*) with the comparative clumsiness of the writing for the
previous Roll of Honour (pages 70–1).

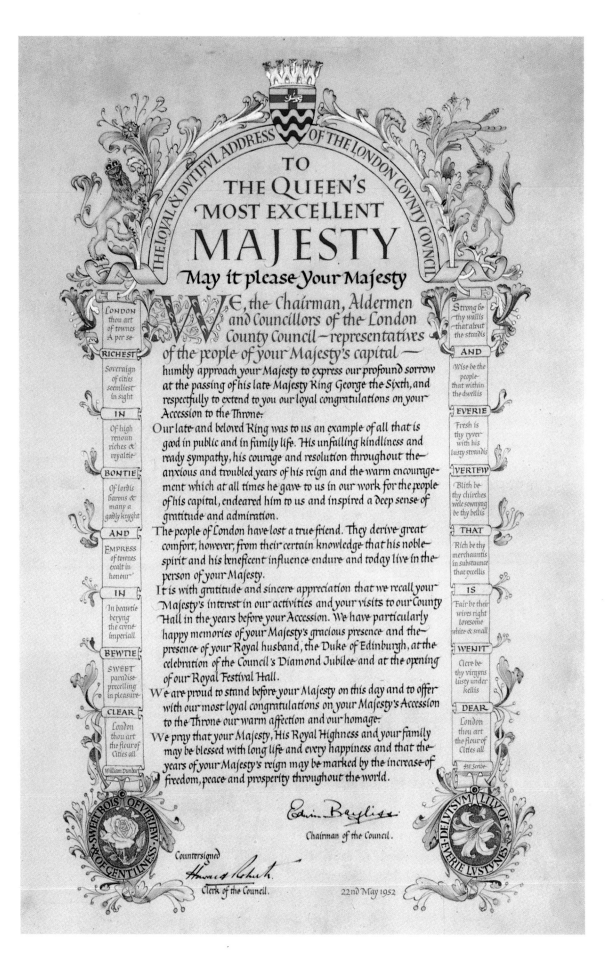

THE LOYAL & DVTIFVL ADDRESS OF THE LONDON COUNTY COUNCIL

TO THE QUEEN'S MOST EXCELLENT MAJESTY

May it please Your Majesty

WE, the Chairman, Aldermen and Councillors of the London County Council — representatives of the people of your Majesty's capital —

humbly approach your Majesty to express our profound sorrow at the passing of his late Majesty King George the Sixth, and respectfully to extend to you our loyal congratulations on your Accession to the Throne.

Our late and beloved King was to us an example of all that is good in public and in family life. His unfailing kindliness and ready sympathy, his courage and resolution throughout the anxious and troubled years of his reign and the warm encouragement which at all times he gave to us in our work for the people of his capital, endeared him to us and inspired a deep sense of gratitude and admiration.

The people of London have lost a true friend. They derive great comfort, however, from their certain knowledge that his noble spirit and his beneficent influence endure and today live in the person of your Majesty.

It is with gratitude and sincere appreciation that we recall your Majesty's interest in our activities and your visits to our County Hall in the years before your Accession. We have particularly happy memories of your Majesty's gracious presence and the presence of your Royal husband, the Duke of Edinburgh, at the celebration of the Council's Diamond Jubilee and at the opening of our Royal Festival Hall.

We are proud to stand before your Majesty on this day and to offer with our most loyal congratulations on your Majesty's Accession to the Throne our warm affection and our homage.

We pray that your Majesty, His Royal Highness and your family may be blessed with long life and every happiness and that the years of your Majesty's reign may be marked by the increase of freedom, peace and prosperity throughout the world.

Edwin Bayliss
Chairman of the Council.

Countersigned
Howard Roberts
Clerk of the Council.

22nd May 1952

LONDON thou art of townes A per se
RICHEST
Soveraign of cities seemliest in sight
IN
Of high renoun riches & royaltie
BONTIE
Of lordis barons & many a gudly knyght
AND
EMPRESS of townes exalt in honour
IN
In beawtie beryng the croun imperiall
BEWTIE
SWEET paradise precelling in pleasure
CLEAR
London thou art the flour of Cities all
William Dunbar

Strong be thy wallis that about the standis
AND
Wise be the people that within the dwellis
EVERIE
Fresh is thy ryver with his lusty strandis
VERTEW
Blith be thy chirches wele sownyng be thy bellis
THAT
Rich be thy merchauntis in substaunce that excellis
IS
Fair be their wives right lovesome white & small
WENIT
Clene be thy virgyns lusty under kellis
DEAR
London thou art the flour of Cities all
W. Scribe

SWEET ROIS OF VERTEW & OF GENTILNES

& DELYTSVM LILY OF EVERIE LVSTYNES

ACCESSION ADDRESS
The White House 1952

Vellum scroll. Written in black ink, vermillion and blue watercolour, with decoration in
raised and burnished gold leaf, powder gold and watercolour.

66 × 40 cm

Irene wrote in a letter: 'I had the first wild idea going home in the train after teaching.
It was to have the Lion and the Unicorn swinging the Garter between them. This was,
of course, altogether too frivolous, but it led to the architectural design calling to mind very
early (10th century English) traditional work. Both side borders carry the poem of the
Scottish poet William Dunbar "In praise of the City of London".'

The design is essentially architectural, and the side scrolls appear at first to be columns.
The inherent problem of the 'columns' seeming to float in space without foundations to
stand on has been elegantly resolved: the tops are capitals, but as the eye travels downwards,
the columns turn into ribbons from which hang the medallions.

Details of Medallions

Irene's letter continues: 'The medallions at the base line were by the same poet "In Praise
of a Lady", likening her to a Lily and a Rose. I came to realise that the medallions, while
originally circles, would, as flattened ovals, give a greater sense of weight to steady the ribbon
of the side wings. The LCC shield was brought in as the keystone to the arch.'

HOPEFUL BEGINNING:
collage
The White House 1951

Double opening, bound in
brown marbled Cockerell paper,
with brown cloth spine. Includes
scraps from over forty pieces of
work, plus one word of Irene's
mother's writing (Omnipotent)
and letterheads from Lord and
Lady Cholmondeley's notepaper.
Sent as Christmas Greetings to
the Cholmondeleys.

42 × 28 cm

In much calligraphic work, the
design and the arrangement of the
lettering within it aid the reading
of the text: the hierarchy of
weights and scales of words
develop the narrative sequence.
Here, however, there is no logical
thread. It is pure compositional
play. The eye can wander freely
round from writing to drawing in
any order. Note how fluid the
design is (maybe because of the
diagonals?). The eye is always
kept on the move, so that it does
not get locked into one place.
Thus the whole page is being
constantly reviewed and every
element reincorporated.

to have communication with the fields

Within and out, in and out, round as a ball,
With hither and thither, as straight as a line,
With lily, germander, and sops-in-wine,
With sweet-briar
And bon-fire
And strawberry wire
And columbine.

SING

Run Shepherds Run
where Bethlem blest appears,
children

LITTLE
CHRIST JESUS
OUR BROTHER
IS BORN
will lead
you in at HEAVEN'S
GATE

dead wood.
And the dead wood will be cast into the fire.

Faith is a cathedral rooted
in the soil of France
Charity is a hospital, an almshouse
which gathers up all the miseries
of the world

Charity

And they cried out in a loud voice

"He made us!"

APPROACH

Omnipotent

I LOVE

days of old—

This was written by my
Julia Elizabeth Bass
mother,
as a girl.

affectionate memento
avec tendresse
la maison
FRANCE

BASS
Le Roc
GOLFE JUAN
A.M.

MEMORY OF

FRIENDSHIP IS IN LOVING RATHER THAN IN BEING LOV'D
WHICH IS ITS MUTUAL BENEDICTION AND RECOMPENSE

CONTINUE

Run

Fierce

Il y en a une qui est
sweet as the fruit clear as the horn

Calligraphy is distinguished by harmony of style. It is conscious of the methods by which it gets its results. Its forms are definite.

Calligraphy is distinguished by harmony of style. It is conscious of the methods by which it gets its results. Its forms are definite.

CALLIGRAPHY IS DISTINGUISHED
The White House 1951

Black ink on vellum.
28 × 22 cm (*approx*)

This was written to replace 'Little Gidding', which had not reproduced well, in Alfred Fairbank's *A Book of Scripts*. These four trials (of at least sixteen versions Irene did on both vellum and paper) show the rigorous criticism she applied to her own work, especially that done for reproduction. Her notes speak for themselves.

Calligraphy
is distinguished by
harmony of style.
It is conscious of the
methods by which
it gets its results.
Its forms are definite.

Calligraphy
is distinguished by
harmony of style.
It is conscious of the
methods by which
it gets its results.
Its forms are definite

On Vellum, 1st Trial: decision to return to pencil B planning ~ abandoned because edges not clean or sharp enough for reproduction ~ also the size of the letters and the texture of line vary ~ especially line 4.

2nd Trial: the "g" in Calligraphy oozed ~ or the skin wd. not take the ink at the first touch of the pen in this letter: dislike of capital "I" with gothic flick in line 4: not satisfied with sweetness of form or rhythm last line too stiff & too close in texture.

3rd Trial: a lost rhythm in Calligraphy: all the writing livelier because of the resistant surface of the vellum & the pen could grip the surface. but, although these points were good the whole was spoilt as the skin was too porous allowing the ink to spread. Surface a little like horny blotting paper, (of such an apparent contradiction may be suggested as an example) the surface shd. be matt & velvety ~ pen making a "trough" to curb & contain the ink

4th Trial The letter "t" in distinguished & b in "by" line 1 (& the letter 'f' not so good in any line. The f is not crossed through the stem & the base of every 's' is short. too short. The surface is not sympathetic it gives an oozed letter rather than a "crisp" letter clean at the edges. This particular vellum surface was chosen for use for reproduction purposes since less fine lines reproduce more truly but the surface

affects the control of the pen in the wrong way instead of aiding the hand and pen. Faults wh. are acceptable in long (or short) REAL MSS. carried by the life of the writing & the finesse of pen touch in an original MS are not acceptable in such a short text for reproduction accep

These all went
wrong
not really easy free.

paper too harsh.

prob all too
wordy

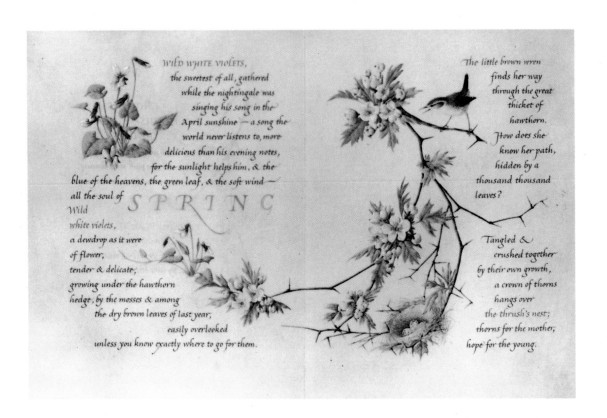

QUARTET OF THE SEASONS
The White House 1955–61

Illustrated by Marie Angel, and written by Irene Wellington. This book was commissioned by Philip Hofer of the Harvard University Library and subsequently given by him to the Bodleian Library, Oxford. Watercolour and ink on vellum.
23 × 35 cm (*double opening*)

The book was to be bound in separate folds of vellum, but this was never done. The double openings each portray a season (although there are two alternative versions for summer, and winter secures only a single page).

The designs of the double openings are quite different from each other, and are thought of each as a single panel rather than two separate pages. Each opening was treated as an entity in its own right, unlike most manuscript books which have a unifying framework that runs throughout the book.

A QUARTET
OF THE SEASONS

the sweet violets bloom a-fresh

THE SHEAF YOU

every spring on the mounds, the cowslips come

MAY TAKE HOME

and the happy note of the cuckoo, the wild rose

WITH YOU·BUT

of mid-summer & the golden wheat of August

THE WIND THAT

it is the same beautiful old country

WAS AMONG IT

al·ways new.

STAYS WITHOUT

A.

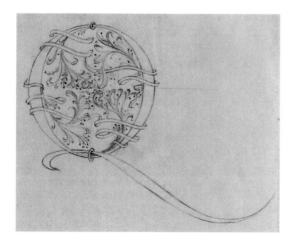

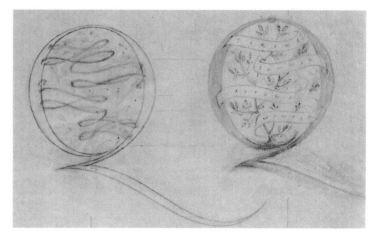

Trials and tracings for title page
Originally the book was to be called 'A Herbal for Philip Hofer', and only later was the
title changed to Quartet of the Seasons. Here is an example of how a multitude of ideas
can be worked through and discarded before arriving at the final solution, which may be,
as in this case, quite different and much simpler than the first sketch. The four rough drafts
shown here are taken from a sheaf of about twenty. The last one (*above*) is the final version
on vellum.

ALPHABETICAL FRAGMENTS
The White House 1957

A collage compiled of extracts from other calligraphic pieces, arranged and combined 'for fun' on a background of S M Cockerell combed paper, to give a sense of richness.

45.5 × 61 cm

In a note, Irene explained the sources of the fragments; her comments are in italic: from top left corner, moving down: 'A Bqlir Chesterdrores' (a peculiar chest of drawers), 'a butcher's book', and 'Moreover, if the spelling of a word . . .' are all quotations from 'Come Hither' by Walter de la Mare, and *is a trial run for a page of a future Copybook, circa 1958*. The raven is from the design for the title page of the Brockley County School Roll of Honour (1939–45). 'This is the living thing . . .', a sonnet by John Masefield from a MS book written for a surgeon in Edinburgh; photostat of 'dainty harts' taken from the title page, circa 1943; this text was written especially for the panel.

Top centre of the panel: IW monogram with turkey quills and squirrels is *a Signature tune scribbled for John Farleigh's book The Creative Craftsman*. Underneath: 'Write faster, mind your p's and q's . . .' is the title page of The Irene Wellington Copy Book, No. III. 'Praise for Brother Fire', circa 1935, is *a version from a book on vellum of St Francis's "Song of the Creatures", written in exchange for a complete set of tools and presses for bookbinding. For Florence McLeod, mountain climber, bookbinder, nurse in Serbia 1914'*. Top right: a *'simple lower case alphabet from my Copy Book No. I'*.

a b c d e f g h i j k l m n o p q r s t u v w x y z

It's a very odd thing – As odd as can be –

MISS T.

That what – ever Miss T. eats
Turns into Miss T.;
Porridge and apples,
Mince muf fins & mutton,
Jam, junket, jumbles –
Not a rap, not a button
It matters; the moment
They're out of her plate,
Tho' shared by Miss Butcher
And sour Mr. Bate;
Tiny & cheer ful,
And neat as can be,
Whatever Miss T. eats
whatever Turns into Miss T.

P.S.

Porridge & apples,
Mince, & muffins & mutton,
Jam, junket, & jumbles

a b c d e f g   f g
h i j k l m n
o p q r r r s t   s t
w x y z   u v

Irene Wellington

xyz

The arrangement is extremely uninhibited and free from conventional theories of design. The choice of elements and manner of putting them together is personal. So this is a format that cannot be copied. It comes only from within. Freed from the responsibilities of the exacting standards of craftsmanship so forcibly instilled by Johnston, it was in the medium of collage that Irene was best able to realize her compositional gifts and her delight in complexity. Perhaps more than any other piece of Irene's work, this one has stretched our ideas of the scope and possibilities of calligraphy. Even today, when expressive freedom in work is more widely seen and accepted, this piece still seems adventurous. In 1957, it was exceptional.

Underneath: 'It's a very odd thing – As odd as can be . . .' is '*a version of Walter de la Mare's poem "Miss T" also to be found in my Copy Book No. III, here written especially for this panel*'. The Foundational Hand alphabet is '*after EJ, an alphabet written for a class of formal calligraphy*'. The footprint is '*an imprint of my own foot, a trial run (as it were) for a framed vellum panel of Alice Meynell's essay "Near the Ground" now in the collection of the Marchioness of Cholmondeley. Note: my heel has trodden on my own signature.*' The drawing of a foal, 'A thing so honey-coloured and so tall', is a fragment of an etching executed at the RCA, 1929. The large signature underneath is from the cover of the Copybooks.

THE BAILIFFS OF LYDD
London 1972–3

Panel on vellum.
86.5 × 104 cm

This was Irene's last major work. It was commissioned by the Borough of Lydd and hangs in the Guildhall there, together with the panel she did as a tribute to her father (The Borough of Lydd, pages 106–7).

It is extremely difficult to arrange such a mass of information, comprising neary 400 names of differing lengths with their dates, and listed under their appropriate monarchs. In fact, nothing can be more boring than a list of names. But Irene has made of it a beautiful piece of abstract design. She used the device of the gold crowns to give a sparkle to the piece, and to break up the columns.

Note that, in the band of lettering at the top, there is no line spacing. The lines of letters are allowed to touch each other, forming a decorative frieze. This is of particular interest, as Irene was being influenced here by the work of a younger generation of calligraphers (who had in turn perhaps been influenced by David Jones). It shows that she is still open to new ideas, still able to adapt and change.

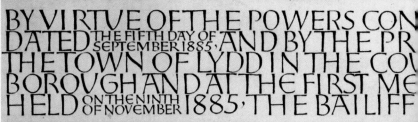

...S WHO & SERVED LYDD AND THEIR SOVEREIGN

MCCCCXXVII 14 27 · MDCCCLXXXV 18 85

...istration & authority in a particular district - generally a KING's officer, especially the chief administrator of a HUNDRED.

1630-1631	Peter Maplisden
1631 32	William Godfrey
1632 33	Stephen Browne
1633 34	Thomas Stroughill Jnr.
1634 35	Thomas Bate, Snr.
1635 38	Three years unrecorded
1638 39	John Glover
1639 40	Clement Tipp
1640-1642	Two years unrecorded
1642 43	Richard Glover
1643 44	Thomas Stroughill
1644 45	Clement Tipp
1645 46	Richard Bate
1646 47	Richard Glover
1647 50	Three years unrecorded
1648 CHARLES II 1685	
1650-1651	Stephen Durrant
1651 52	Stephen Durrant
1652 53	Edward Ashie
1653 54	Richard Kennett
1654 55	Richard Bate
1655 56	Richard Bate
1656 57	Thomas Higginson
1657 58	James Bate
1658 59	John Stroughill
1659 60	Edward Cullemben
1660-1661	Edward Cullemben
1661 62	John Knight
1662 63	John Bartholomew
1663 64	Michael Chidwick
1664 65	John Bateman
1665 66	John Bateman
1666 67	Thomas Bateman
1667 68	Edward Cullemben
1668 69	Edward Cullemben
1669 70	Edward Cullemben
1670-1671	William Sudell
1671 72	William Sudell
1672 73	John Bateman
1673 74	Henry Potter
1674 75	William Sudell
1675 76	William Sudell
1676 77	William Glover
1677 78	William Glover
1678 79	John Barton
1679 80	John Barton
1680-1681	John Barton
1681 82	William Ringsmill
1682 83	John Bateman
1683 84	Humphrey Lee
1684 85	William Sudell
1685 JAMES II 1688	
1685 86	Edward Cullemben
1686 87	John Bateman
1687 88	William Edmunds
1688 89	Thomas Godfrey
1689 WILLIAM & MARY 1702	
1689 90	William Wing
1690-1691	William Edmunds
1691 92	John Skinner
1692 93	John Skinner
1693 94	William Edmunds
1694 95	Nicholas Pyne
1695 96	William Edmunds
1696 97	John Skinner
1697 98	John Skinner
1698 99	John Jorden
1699 1700	Samuel Mittell
1700-1701	Samuel Mittell
1701 14	Thirteen yrs unrecorded
1702 ANNE 1714	
1714 GEORGE I 1727	
1714 15	Thomas Bateman
1715 16	John Skinner
1716 18	Two years unrecorded
1718 19	Thomas Bateman
1719 20	One year unrecorded
1720-1721	Thomas Bateman
1721 25	Four years unrecorded
1725 26	Thomas Plummer
1726 29	Three yrs unrecorded
1727 GEORGE II 1760	
1729 30	Charles Coxsell
1730-1731	Thomas Bateman
1731 32	John Lee
1732 33	James Bannewell
1733 34	Charles Coxsell
1734 35	Thomas Bateman
1735 36	John Lee
1736 37	James Bannewell
1737 38	Charles Coxsell
1738 39	Mark Skinner / Thomas Bateman
1739 40	John Lee
1740-1741	James Bannewell
1741 42	Charles Coxsell
1742 43	Thomas Bateman
1743 44	William Temple
1744 45	Mark Skinner
1745 46	John Lee
1746 47	Thomas Portman / Thomas Cobb
1747 48	William Temple
1748 49	Mark Skinner
1749 50	John Lee
1750-1751	William Temple
1751 52	William Temple
1752 53	Mark Skinner
1753 54	John Lee
1754 55	John Plummer
1755 56	John Plummer
1756 57	Thomas Denne
1757 58	William Temple / Mark Skinner
1758 59	Thomas Denne
1759 60	John Plummer
1760 GEORGE III 1820	
1760-1761	Mark Skinner
1761 62	James Brett
1762 63	John Skinner
1763 64	Mark Skinner
1764 65	John Shoosmith
1765 66	William Waylett
1766 67	James Brett
1767 68	Robert Cobb
1768 69	John Shoosmith
1769 70	William Waylett
1770-1771	Robert Cobb
1771 72	Robert Cobb
1772 73	John Shoosmith
1773 74	William Waylett
1774 75	Robert Cobb
1775 76	John Shoosmith
1776 77	William Waylett
1777 78	Richard Denne
1778 79	Robert Cobb
1779 80	John Shoosmith
1780-1781	Rev. John Goodwin
1781 82	William Waylett
1782 83	Richard Denne
1783 84	Robert Cobb
1784 85	John Shoosmith
1785 86	Rev. John Goodwin
1786 87	William Waylett
1787 88	Robert Cobb
1788 89	John Shoosmith
1789 90	Rev. John Goodwin
1790-1791	David Denne
1791 92	William Waylett
1792 93	Robert Cobb
1793 94	Rev. John Goodwin
1794 95	David Denne
1795 96	William Waylett
1796 97	Robert Cobb
1797 98	Rev. John Goodwin
1798 99	William Waylett
1799 1800	Robert Cobb
1800-1801	Rev. John Goodwin
1801 02	William Waylett
1802 03	Robert Cobb
1803 04	Rev. John Goodwin
1804 05	Rev. John Goodwin
1805 06	Robert Cobb
1806 07	Benjamin Denne
1807 08	David Denne
1808 09	Benjamin Cobb
1809 10	Benjamin Cobb
1810-1811	Benjamin Cobb
1811 12	Benjamin Cobb
1812 13	Benjamin Cobb
1813 14	Benjamin Cobb
1814 15	Henshaw Russell
1815 16	Benjamin Cobb
1816 17	Benjamin Cobb
1817 18	Gilbert Robinson
1818 19	Benjamin Cobb
1819 20	David Denne
1820 GEORGE IV 1830	
1820-1821	David Denne
1821 22	Henshaw Russell
1822 23	David Denne
1823 24	Henshaw Russell
1824 25	David Denne
1825 26	Henshaw Russell
1826 27	David Denne
1827 28	David Denne
1828 29	David Denne
1829 30	John Robinson
1830 WILLIAM IV 1837	
1830-1831	David Denne
1831 32	David Denne
1832 33	John Robinson
1833 34	David Denne
1834 35	Gilbert Wm. Robinson
1835 36	John Robinson
1836 37	David Denne
1837 VICTORIA 1901	
1837 38	John Robinson
1838 39	David Denne
1839 40	John Robinson
1840-1841	David Denne
1841 42	John Robinson
1842 43	David Denne
1843 44	John Robinson
1844 45	David Denne
1845 46	John Robinson
1846 47	David Denne
1847 48	John Robinson
1848 49	David Denne
1849 50	John Robinson
1850-1851	David Denne
1851 52	Stephen Burgess
1852 53	David Denne
1853 54	Stephen Burgess
1854 55	David Denne
1855 56	David Denne
1856 57	David Denne
1857 58	James Rolfe
1858 59	David Denne
1859 60	Stephen Burgess
1860-1861	Edwin Cock
1861 62	Edwin Cock
1862 63	George Finn
1863 64	Alured Denne
1864 65	James Rolfe
1865 66	Thomas Finn
1866 67	James Rolfe
1867 68	James Rolfe
1868 69	Alured Denne
1869 70	Thomas Finn
1870-1871	James Rolfe
1871 72	Thomas Finn
1872 73	Edward Thomas Bass
1873 74	Edward Thomas Bass
1874 75	Edward Thomas Bass
1875 76	Thomas Finn
1876 77	Thomas Finn
1877 78	Thomas Finn
1878 79	Edwin Finn
1879 80	Edward Thomas Bass
1880-1881	Thomas Finn
1881-1885	Edwin Finn
	final four years

...ne hundred hides: "hixe" - a sq. measure of land...100 acres; sufficient to support one family & household - Old English hid, higid hiw...

At Lydd & New Romney, companies of players from fourteen neighbouring towns & villages entertained in the local records, stretching from a year or so before, to eight years after, the fifteenth century. These plays are not only a primitive religious drama, born of the church & its feasts: they are the genuine expression of the town life of the English people when it was still lived with some exuberance of spirits & communal pleasure. Hardly a town but had its own particular play, acted for the people in the street or churchyard or before dignitaries & their brethren sitting in state in the Church or Town Hall. Lydd's own special plays were "St. George" & the inter-lude of our Lord's Passion.

The corn is sown again, it grows; the stars burn out, the darkness goes; The rhythms change, they do not close.

...thur Finn in 1911: also from the Minutes of HUNDRED Courts & various other Archives in the custody of the Lydd Borough Council

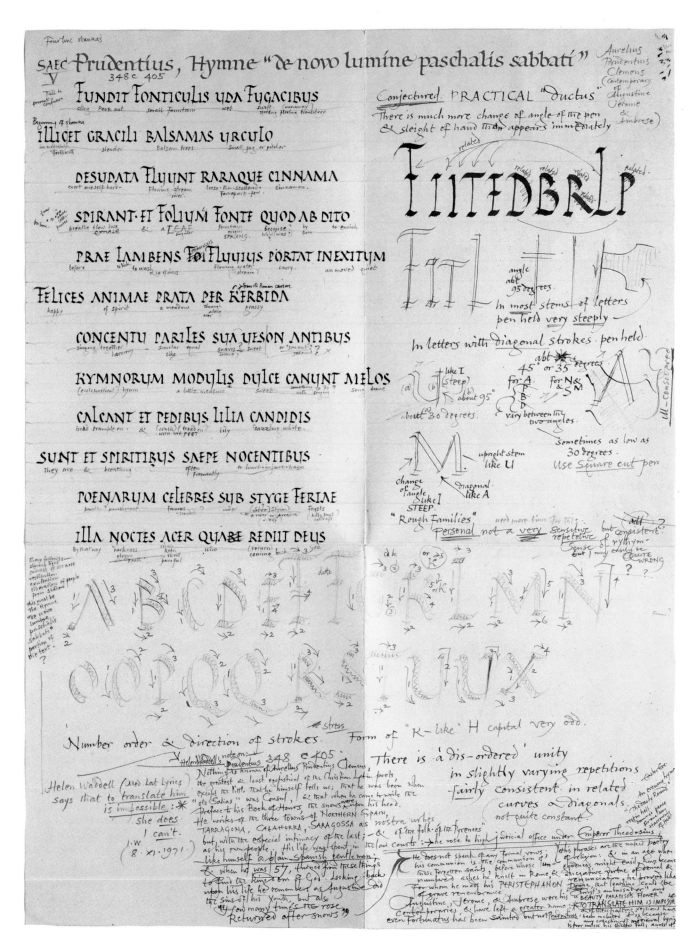

THE
SOCIETY OF
SCRIBES
AND
ILLUMINATORS
FIFTIETH
ANNIVERSARY
1921
1971

MCM
XXI

MCM
LXXI

"EVERY SCRIBE / WHICH IS INSTRUCTED / UNTO THE KINGDOM / OF HEAVEN IS LIKE UNTO / A MAN THAT IS AN / HOUSE-HOLDER / WHICH BRINGETH / FORTH OUT OF HIS / TREASURE THINGS / NEW AND OLD" Chapter 13 St Matthew

A B C X Y Z

(LEFT)
SSI FIFTIETH
ANNIVERSARY
BROCHURE
London 1971

Brown ink printed on beige card.
21 × 15.5 cm

Anyone who has ever attempted to do scroll-work round an underlying oval shape will be aware of the difficulties. Although the shape of the individual scrolls appears to be the same, each one has had to be subtly altered to suit its placing in the pattern.

(OPPOSITE)
PRUDENTIUS: rustic capitals
panel
London 1971

Inks and pencil on paper.
51 × 38 cm

Living in London at this time provided Irene with the opportunity for further study. She attended Professor Julian Brown's lectures on palaeography. She was able to bring the experience of a life-time as a calligrapher to bear upon the problem of analysing an historic letter form. This sheet shows how she painstakingly explored the subject, reliving each stroke of the pen and noting her discoveries as she went.

Characteristically, she responded in a highly personal way, reaching out to the poet, Prudentius, whose words they were, and to the translator, Helen Waddell, quoting her notes on him.

Irene was so conscientious a student that, when she mistakenly thought she was to translate as well as analyse the script, she spent hours dredging up the memories of her school-girl Latin in the attempt. She was greatly relieved to find that Helen Waddell said 'to translate him is impossible'.

UNIVERSITY OF DA

DALHOUSIE UNIVE

NIVERSITY COLLEGE OF TH

UNIVERSITY OF HON

UNIVERSITY COLLEGE, 1

UNIVERSITY COLLEGE OF K

UNIVERSITY OF LUC

UNIVERSITY OF MA

MAKERERE COLLEGE, KA

UNIVERSITY OF MAL

ROYAL UNIVERSITY OF (

UNIVERSITY OF MELBO

UNIVERSITY OF NA

On this and the following pages are detailed examples of some of Irene's different styles of writing.

UNCIALS: Institute of Commonwealth Studies (*detail*)
The White House 1952

Rough. Black ink on paper.

Classical forms were always a rich source of inspiration for Irene, from which she could 'breed varieties' to suite her own purposes. This script is based on an Uncial hand found in early Christian manuscripts.
For this piece, Irene was perhaps seeking the formality and inscriptional quality that a capital

ut what shal I seye of

en, that neitherknowen

hem as heye as the heve

they comen to any wik

destruccions as doth tl

han the flambe walw

armes.

be that dignitees and.

e thing is full selde, w

nitees and powers, but

(LEFT)
COMPRESSED HAND:
detail of writing from the rough
for The Borough of Lydd
The White House 1948

Black ink on paper.

This characteristic hand of Irene's is similar to the writing used in 'Upon being given a Norfolk Turkey' on which Irene comments: 'A compressed easy hand not Gothic, not italic, not quite compressed foundational, too easy in the arches for that . . .' Most of the 'recognition factors' in letters are in the upper half of the letter form (cover up the bottom half of a line of writing, and it can still be read easily; cover up the top half and reading becomes difficult. Also there are more letters with sprung arches at the top (m, n, h, r, etc.) than at the bottom (a, u, etc.). Here, Irene has achieved the best of both worlds. The arches of m, n, etc., are rounded, giving a feeling of strength, and the more diagonal lift of the u and a gives a sense of movement and grace. Try turning it upside down: the letters will appear heavy at the bottom.

Although the beginner is encouraged to try and relate these two arches, so that they conform to an underlying ideal shape, eventually each person will develop his or her individual script. This only comes into being after rigorous analysis and understanding of letters, combined with much practice. As in any discipline (for instance, playing a musical instrument), the rules have to be learned, absorbed and then let go.

letter form gives, but without the stiffness that can occur when capital letters stand individually on a line without touching each other.

The rounded pen shapes of an Uncial have a written rather than a drawn quality, and Irene has given the letters a steeper (and more natural) pen angle than is usual in most historic examples of this script, so that they have a greater fluency and grace. She has also adapted some of the letter forms themselves (note, for instance, the minuscule e and y, and the less archaic form of D) which gives the writing a more modern appearance. It is an extremely intelligent solution to a universal calligraphic problem: how to take an historical model and revitalize it so that it sits happily in the twentieth century. Here, Irene has magically blended the dignity of a majuscule with the fluency of a miniscule.

We shall not cease from exploration
And the end of all our exploring
Will be to arrive where we started
And to know the place for the first time.
Through the unknown, remembered gate
When the last of earth left to discover
Is that which was the beginning;
At the source of the longest river
The voice of the hidden waterfall
And the children in the apple-tree
Not known, because not looked for
But heard, half-heard in the stillness

Between two waves of the sea.
Quick now, here, now, always—
A condition of complete simplicity

ut Love, all seeing, though painted Blind,
akes wisdom live in a woman's mind.
is love knew well from her own heart's Bleeding
he word of help that her man was needing;
nd there she stood with her eyes most Bright,
eady to cheer her heart's delight.

he said, "My darling, I feel so proud
o see you followed By all the crowd;
nd I shall be proud as I see you win.
ight Royal, Soyland and Peterkin
re the three I pick, first, second, third.
nd oh, now listen to what I heard.
ust now in the park Sir Norman Cooking
aid, 'Harding, how well Right Royal's looking.
hey've brought him on in the ring, they say.'
ohn said, 'Sir Norman, today's his day.'
nd Sir Norman said, 'If I had a monkey
'd put it on yours, for he looks so spunky.

o you see that the experts think as you.
ow, my own, own, own, may your dream come true;
s I know it will, as I know it must;
ou have all my prayer and my love and trust.

Black ink on hand‑made paper.

Compare the writing with that on the Borough of Lydd panel (pages 106–7). Even though the lightness and openness give this book hand a more informal appearance, it still has a strong familiarity with the hand seen in the Borough of Lydd piece.

Black ink on vellum.
20 × 15.5 cm

This is one of three very similar rejects. (Irene said there were originally thirteen rejects, on both vellum and paper.) They were done for the King Penguin *Book of Scripts* by Alfred Fairbank, and the final version was reproduced in the first and second editions. For the following editions, Irene wrote a passage in larger writing (see 'Calligraphy is distinguished', pages 114–15) which she felt would reproduce more clearly.

The writing was done on the flesh side of the vellum because the very fine lines made by the pen on the hair side of the vellum might be too subtle to reproduce well.

Although the essential shape underlying the letters is a circle and (unlike the oval which an italic hand is based on) the circle is a pure unchangeable form, there is still room for considerable personal interpretation.

SONG OF THE SHIP
Edinburgh 1942

Black ink, blue and red
watercolour on paper.

Various styles of writing skilfully
combined in one piece without
conflict.

HERE COMES a ship a-sailing

With angels flying fast;
[s]he bears a splendid cargo
  And has a mighty mast.

[t]his ship is fully laden,
  Right to her highest board;
[s]he bears the Son from heaven,
  God's high eternal Word.

[up]on the sea unruffled
  The ship moves in to shore,
[to] bring us all the riches
  She has within her store.

[an]d that ship's name is Mary
  Of flowers the rose is she,
[an]d brings to us her baby
  From sin to set us free.

[the] ship made in this fashion,
  In which such store was cast,
[her] sail is love's sweet passion
  The holy Ghost her mast.

In that poor stable   Fléchier, trans.
how charming Jesus lies,   by
    Words are not able   Maurice F. Bell
To fathom his emprise!
No palace of a King
Can show so rare a thing
In history or fable
As that of which we sing
    In that poor stable.
    See here God's power
In weakness fortifies
    This infant hour
Of love's epiphanies!
Our foe is now despoiled,
The wiles of hell are foiled;
On earth there grows a flower
Pure, undefiled, unsoiled —
    See here God's power!
    Though far from knowing
The babe's divinity,
    Mine eyes are growing
To see his majesty;
For lo! the new-born child
Upon me sweetly smiled,
The gift of faith bestowing;
Thus I my Lord descry,
    Though far from knowing
    No more affliction!
For God endures our pains;
    In crucifixion
The Son victorious reigns.
For us the sufferer brings
Salvation in his wings;
To win our soul's affection
Could he, the King of kings,
    Know more affliction?

INFORMAL ITALIC: Irene
Wellington Copybook (*detail*)
The White House *c*. 1955

Black ink on paper. Rejected
trial.

Irene wrote at the beginning of
the Omnibus edition of her
Copybooks that 'The models in
this book are meant to be a
beginning, not an end. By hard
practice we realise the ever-
increasing joy of writing. First
make a thorough study of the
essential shapes. This knowledge,
combined in heart, mind and
hand offers you a spring-board to
the discovery of a personal hand.
Freedom – your own freedom –
has to grow from personal
movements. You will see, coming
up under your eyes, a hand
through the rhythm of the
springing of the arches of the m,
n, and h and the run of the r. Go
ahead and let the letters move
forward, dancing, their feet
scarcely touching the ground!'

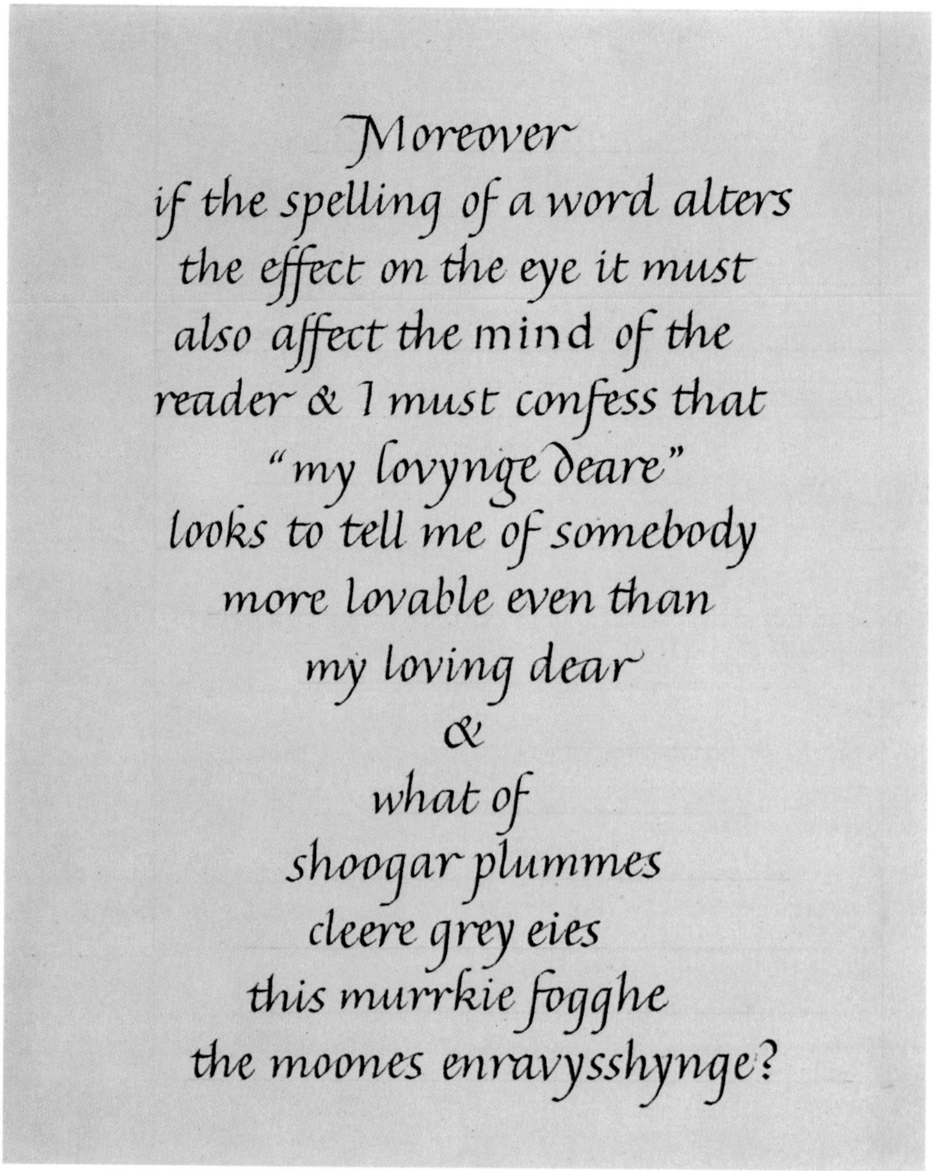

*Moreover
if the spelling of a word alters
the effect on the eye it must
also affect the mind of the
reader & I must confess that
"my lovynge deare"
looks to tell me of somebody
more lovable even than
my loving dear
&
what of
shoogar plummes
cleere grey eies
this murrkie fogghe
the moones enravysshynge?*

(OPPOSITE: CENTRE AND BELOW)
HANDWRITING: Postcards
sent to Ida Henstock
Steep 1975

Two postcards, written with red, blue and green ballpoints.
6.5 × 14 cm; 8.5 × 14 cm

To Irene, ballpoint pens presented possibilities just as any other writing instruments did,
and she enjoyed them for what they were. She loved to write in different colours, and these
pens afforded instant opportunities to do so. Many people have treasured cards from her,
such as those shown above. The carefully chosen words, written with such spontaneous
generosity of spirit, often appeared at just the right moment.

The teacher is the real hope, the vital link between the pupil & the many existing examples of cursive writing from the past as well as the models offered in this, his own day, the best of which are based in history & suitable if considered as a "spring board" to free individual cursive.

Edward Johnston
But, that master of calligraphy with characteristic perception wrote: "But if an alphabet be written as a SPECIMEN it is primarily a specimen Alphabet (and is debarred from that natural freedom or run of free writing— Brushed by the feather's of an Angel's wing in passing—

To IDA with love from Irene   April 1975·
Flat 2, Ashford Chace, Steep, Petersfield, Hampshire   Petersfield (0730) 2096
                    WHERE IS TRUTH.
What is truth, my darling,
Where is truth, my dear,   Poem by my friend
    It's an aspect of the sun   Joy FINZI.
        & the shadow beneath the weir   widow of
What is love, my dearest,   Gerald Finzi
And where can it be found.   composer &
    It is the warmth by which we live   musician
        & as dew upon the ground.

P.S.
    I hope you will soon be over this present
wretched & grievous patch. afterwards
after going through "the shadow under the weir"
    I do believe one is better able to see
perhaps strangely enough one of the many
aspects of the sun perhaps its warmth·

writing on lap, legs up, can't look out a little
strip of skin (vellum) to do a proper book mark
even with steel pen (nib)

(LEFT)
HANDWRITING:
Dossier A-Z 73
London 1973

Detail from printed book.

This passage comes from an article specially written for a Belgian publication, *Dossier A-Z Typographique Internationale*. Selected people were asked to reply to questions relating to writing, lettering and typography. In her answer, Irene stated that she felt handwriting should be 'a living thing'. Whatever the starting point or model used (whether it be an Anglo-Saxon gloss or Humanist italic) it should serve as a spring-board and should develop 'spontaneously in the actual "doing" (almost as a matter of course) fulfilling an immediate need'. Above all, she felt the act of writing should be enjoyed. Irene's own handwriting reflects this joy of movement and rhythm. She kept a selection of old and favourite fountain pens and has used one of them here. Even though the writing has a greater formality than her usual hand (as she thought appropriate for publication) it still has remarkable freedom and life. One can sense the vital human touch behind it.

SSI FIFTIETH ANNIVERSARY MOTIF

IRENE WELLINGTON

A CHRONOLOGY

29 October 1904	Born Irene Bass at Lydd, Kent.
1916–21	Attended Ashford County School, Kent.
1921–5	Attended Maidstone School of Art, Kent.
1925	Won a Royal Exhibition scholarship to the Royal College of Art, London.
1925–30	Attended Royal College of Art.
1926–7	Suffered nervous breakdown; absent from RCA.
1927–30	Assistant to Edward Johnston in calligraphy class.
1929	Elected Craft Member of the Society of Scribes and Illuminators.
11 September 1930	Married Ernest John (Jack) Sutton at Lydd; moved to Edinburgh, where he was living.
1932–43	Part-time teacher in writing and illuminating at Edinburgh College of Art.
1943	Left Jack Sutton and filed a petition for the annulment of the marriage.
1943–4	Shared a flat in Primrose Hill, London.
September 1944	Marriage annulled.
11 November 1944	Married Hubert Wellington and moved to The White House, Henley on Thames, Oxon.
1944–59	Part-time teacher at the Central School of Arts and Crafts, London.
1945–7	Assistant Instructor at the Royal College of Art.
1967	Hubert Wellington died.
1969	Moved to Palace Garden Mews, London.
1974	Moved to Steep, Hants.
1976	Returned to Lydd, Kent.
1982	Suffered a stroke and was taken to Ashford Hospital.
1983	Transferred to Wray Common Nursing Home, Reigate, Surrey.
18 September 1984	Died.

IRENE WELLINGTON

MAIN WORKS

MAIDSTONE SCHOOL OF ART 1921–5

1925   The Defence of Guenevere (*illuminated double opening*)

        The Litany (*illuminated book*)

ROYAL COLLEGE OF ART 1925–30

c. 1927   On the Graces and Anxieties of Pig-Driving (*book*)

c. 1927–30   The Golden Age (The Olympians) (*book*)

1928   The Rime of the Ancient Mariner (*book*)

1929   Mare and Foal (*etching*)

TOURNEY HALL 1930

1930   Beloved, Let Us Love One Another (*book*)

EDINBURGH 1930–43

1930–31   Oxfordshire and Buckinghamshire Light Infantry Roll of Honour, 1914–18

1934   Diary (26 Days and 25 Nights of Summer) (*book*)

1935   Women's Guild of the Church of Scotland (*presentation scroll*)

1936   Hawick Parish Church: Roll of the Ministry

c. 1936   Bells have Wide Mouths and Tongues (*panel*)

1936–7   The Tower of London (*illustrated double opening*)

1937   Sir Alexander Grant Presentation (*book*)

c. 1937   Bristo Church (*book*)

1939–42   Del Tumbeor Nostre Dame (illustrated by Sax Shaw) (*book*)

1940   Give Me the Wings of Faith (*book*)

1941   For the Absolute Good ('S' for Edward Johnston) (*small unbound book*)

1942   The Song of the Ship (*double opening on paper*)

        The Violet (Deep Springs of Happiness) (*vellum fold*)

        Hubert Wellington Appreciation (*double opening on vellum*)

1942–3   Awake Thou Wintry Earth (*book*)

        Frank Rushforth Presentation (*double opening on vellum*)

1943   My Heart is like a Singing Bird (*birthday card*)

c. 1943   The Darkling Thrush (*book*)

        Song of the Creatures (Brother Fire) (*illustrated book*)

c. 1943–4   Canongate Parish Church (*presentation inscription*)

Dainty Harts (This is a Living Thing) (*illustrated double opening*)

Undated   Alarms and Excursions (*book*)

For Mortal Men are Blind (*panel*)

I Asked the Earth (*panel*)

Where wast thou when I laid the Foundations of the Earth (*panel*)

LONDON 1943–4

1943   Tehran Dinner (HBM Legation) (*seating plan*)

1944   Dott Memorial Library (*commemorative panel*)

Harry Hopkins Presentation (*small presentation panel*)

Mayor of Andover Presentation (*presentation book*)

THE WHITE HOUSE 1944–69

1945   Professor Sir Patrick Abercrombie Presentation (*presentation book*)

Talk on Edward Johnston at Artworkers Guild, 10 November

1945–7   The Foundational Hand Exemplar

1946   The Worshipful Company of Feltmakers 1939–45 War Record

Rev. Harold Pain (Vicar of Turville, Bucks) (*triptych*)

Paulinus of Nola (*panel*)

1946–8   Imperial College of Science Centenary Volume (*book*)

1947   The Heads of Strong Old Age are Beautiful (*panel*)

Little Gidding (*vellum page*)

Westminster Fire Office Memorial Book

1948   Borough of Lydd (*panel*)

Czech Christmas Carol (*card*)

Just Like One who wants to Learn to Write (*fold-out card*)

Sir Richard Vynne Southwell Presentation

Wykehamist Roll of Honour 1939–45

1948–50   Oxfordshire and Buckinghamshire Light Infantry Roll of Honour, 1939–45

1949   All Craftsmen share A Knowledge (*panel*)

Synopses for a Book on Writing

1950   M. Auriol Presentation from London County Council (*scroll*)

Cholmondeley Handwriting Competition (Eton, Harrow & Winchester) (*book – with additions annually to 1972*)

George VI Patent

Hippocratic Oath (*panel*)

Il faut que France continue (*book*)

Queen Juliana of the Netherlands Presentation from London County Council (*scroll*)

Lo, I have seen the Open Hand of God (*panel*)

Upon being given a Norfolk Turkey (*bound double opening*)

c. 1950	East Africa House (*panel*)
1951	Calligraphy is distinguished (*vellum page*)
	Christmas Greetings (Hopeful Beginnings) (*collage*)
	Hope (I am, says God, Master of the Three Virtues) (*book*)
	Near the Ground (*illustrated panel*)
	The Price of Charity is Thyself (*birthday card*)
	There are Three Simplicities (*book*)
1952	Accession Address (*presentation scroll*)
	Good Friday Headings for *Radio Times*
	I asked the Earth (*book*)
	Institute of Commonwealth Studies (*panel*)
	David Sassoon & Co. (*presentation panel*)
	Sweet Roman Hand (*book jacket*)
1953	Coronation Address (*presentation scroll*)
	Visit to County Hall by HM Queen Elizabeth II (*scroll*)
1953–4	Cursive Handwriting in Practice (*Ms. for book*)
1955–7 (*date published*)	Irene Wellington Copybooks
1955–61	Quartet of the Seasons (illustrated by Marie Angel) (*unbound vellum book*)
1956	Bulganin/Kruschev Address (*presentation*)
1956–7	Right Royal (*unfinished book*)
1957	Alphabetical Fragments (*collage*)
	Hunter Trials (*book*)
	Llandaff Cathedral (*panel*)
c. 1957–60	Downside School: Stokes Memorial Prize (*bookplate*)
1958–9	Book Jacket to *Edward Johnston*, 1st edition by Priscilla Johnston
1960	Foster Gotch Robinson (*illustrated double opening*)
1961	University of Hong Kong/British Council (*book*)
1968	Marquess of Cholmondeley (*small memorial panel*)
Undated	Ellic Howe Book (Script) (*Ms. for book*)
	Brockley County School War Record

LONDON 1969–74

1970	The Millionth Visitor (*presentation inscription*)
1971	SSI 50th Anniversary (*commemorative brochure*)
1972	Chicago Public Library (*presentation inscription*)
1972–3	The Bailiffs of Lydd (*panel*)
1973	Dossier A–Z 73 (*article*)
1975	Book Jacket to *Edward Johnston*, 2nd edition by Priscilla Johnston

LYDD 1976–82

1977	Copybooks: Omnibus edition jacket
Undated	Rye Harbour Lifeboat Memorial (*panel*)

SELECT BIBLIOGRAPHY

A Book of Scripts: Alfred Fairbank: King Penguin 1949; reissued Faber and Faber 1977

The Calligrapher's Handbook: Editor, Heather Child: Faber & Faber 1956; new edition A & C Black 1985; (USA: Pentalic)

The Irene Wellington Copybooks: Omnibus Edition: A & C Black 1979 (USA: Pentalic) (individual Copybooks previously published by James Barrie and Heinemann)

The Creative Craftsman: John Farleigh: G. Bell & Sons 1950 (out of print)

Dossier A–Z 1973: Association Typographique Internationale, Belgium 1973

Formal Penmanship and other papers: Edward Johnston: Editor, Heather Child: Lund Humphries 1971 (USA: Taplinger)

A Heaven-sent Grace: A Profile of Irene Wellington: Nancy Ouchida: privately printed by The Irene Wellington Collection Appeal 1984

Edward Johnston: Priscilla Johnston: Faber & Faber 1959; reissued Barrie & Jenkins 1976

Lessons in Formal Writing: Edward Johnston: Editors Heather Child and Justin Howes: Lund Humphries 1986

Tributes to Edward Johnston: privately published by Maidstone College of Art and The Society of Scribes and Illuminators 1948

Writing & Illuminating, & Lettering: Edward Johnston: John Hogg 1906; reissued Pitman 1948; reissued A & C Black 1983 (USA: Taplinger)

INDEX

Page numbers in *italic* refer to illustrations and captions

Pages 142-3
I ASKED THE EARTH
(St. Augustine) (*detail*)
Edinburgh *c.* 1942
Trial. Black ink on paper.

Page 144 (top)
DOSSIER A-Z 73
Detail from printed book.

Page 144 (bottom)
INSTITUTE OF COMMONWEALTH
STUDIES (*detail*)
Rough. Black ink on paper.

the deeps, and
they answered
seek above us
winds, and th
inhabitants
Anaximenes

e creeping the

e: We are not

asked the fleet

whole air wit

swered me; T

is deceived; A

renewed if it is to stay alive. The perpetual accumul
of past influences calls for constant re-thinking an
adaptation. Now, our machine techniques widen the s
for the teacher in astonishingly stimulating ways with
a wealth of facsimiles & photographic enlargemen
We no longer depend on the engraving tool to provide
with letters to imitate (with a different tool) though
doubt some contempory use of some new writing inst
may change or influence the trend of cursive — the b
type for instance. Still we can soundly turn to the sam
source from which round-hand & copper-plate, after

TRALIAN NATIONAL U
UNIVERSITY OF ADELA
NIVERSITY OF CAPE T
UNIVERSITY OF DACC
DALHOUSIE UNIVERS
SITY COLLEGE OF THE C
NIVERSITY OF HONG K
VERSITY COLLEGE, IBA

The teacher is the real hope,

& the many existing exa

the past as well as the m

the best of which are base

sidered as a "spring boar

Edward Johnston

But that master of calli

ception wrote: "But if an

SPECIMEN it is primar

is debarred from that no

writing — Brushed by the fear

debarred from those varietie

not real faults in free wri

vital link between the pupil

s of cursive writing from

offered in this, his own day,

history & suitable if con-

free individual cursive.

hy with characteristic per-

habet be written as a

a specimen Alphabet (and

al freedom or run of free

of an Angel's wing in passing —

fferences, faults — which are

it becomes by comparison